Grappling with God

with God

Explorations of the Old Testament for personal and small group use

BOOK FOUR

The Word of the Lord

Nick Fawcett

Kevin
Mayhew

First published in 2000 by
KEVIN MAYHEW LTD
Buxhall
Stowmarket
Suffolk IP14 3BW

0 1 2 3 4 5 6 7 8 9

ISBN 1 84003 502 1
Catalogue No 1500334

Cover design by Jonathan Stroulger
Edited by Katherine Laidler
Typesetting by Louise Selfe

Printed and bound in Great Britain

*Dedicated to the memory of the late Rev Dr W. M. S. West,
formerly principal of Bristol Baptist College,
whose wisdom, graciousness and humility
provided so much encouragement during my training for ministry.*

About the author

Nick Fawcett was born in 1957. He studied Theology at Bristol University and Regent's Park College, Oxford. His early years of ministry were spent in Somerset and Lancashire, and from 1989 to 1996 he was Minister of Gas Green Baptist Church, Cheltenham. From November 1996 to June 1999 he served as Toc H Chaplain and Development Officer for Wales and the West of England.

He is now concentrating full time on his career as a writer, proofreader and indexer. His books to date are *No Ordinary Man* (1997), *Prayers For All Seasons* (1998), *Are You Listening?* (1998) and *Getting It Across* (1999), all published by Kevin Mayhew. He has also written the texts for the *Best Loved Choral Melodies Choral Collection* (1999) and had four hymns chosen for inclusion in the Churches Together Millennium Hymn Book *New Start Hymns and Songs* (1999), both also published by Kevin Mayhew.

He lives with his wife, Deborah, and their two young children, Samuel and Katie, in Wellington, Somerset.

Acknowledgements

I am indebted in the writing of this book to my wife, Deborah, for her invaluable help and support; to Katherine Laidler for all the time and work she has put in to editing the manuscript; to Peter Dainty for his invariably constructive comments and criticisms; and to Kevin Mayhew Publishers for the opportunity to put this and other material into print.

Scripture quotations are taken from the New Revised Standard Version of the Bible, copyright 1989 by the Division of Christian Education of the National Council of the Churches of Christ in the USA. Used by permission. All rights reserved.

Proverbs are taken from *The Penguin Book of Proverbs* and *Collins Gem Dictionary of Quotations*. Unless otherwise stated, the source is unknown.

Contents

Introduction _____

Why read the Old Testament? If I had a pound for every time I've been asked that question I would be a rich man indeed. Many people feel that it is superfluous to their requirements; a confusing and sometimes disturbing book which they feel is best left unexplored. And though I believe they are mistaken, I can understand how they reach that conclusion, for there is much in the Old Testament which is difficult to come to terms with – a multitude of passages which can seem either dull, primitive or downright barbaric by Christian standards. It is often hard to reconcile the God we find there with the God we believe has been revealed to us in Jesus Christ.

Yet to abandon the Old Testament because of such difficulties is to deny oneself untold riches. Imagine Christmas or Holy Week without the great words of the prophet Isaiah: 'The people who walked in darkness have seen a great light'; 'He was wounded for our transgressions, crushed for our iniquities; upon him was the punishment that made us whole.' Imagine Good Friday without the unforgettable cry of the Psalmist: 'My God, my God, why have you forsaken me?' Imagine Pentecost without the wonderful vision of Joel: 'Your sons and daughters shall prophesy, your old men shall dream dreams, and your young men shall see visions.' Like it or not, the Christian faith has its roots firmly in the Old Testament, and it is in the light of its pages that, at least in part, the testimony of the New must be interpreted.

The Old Testament, however, has more to offer than simply words of prophecy. It records some of the most unforgettable stories ever told: Noah and the Great Flood, Esau and Jacob, Moses crossing the Red Sea, Samson and Delilah, David and Goliath, Daniel in the lions' den, Shadrach, Meshach and Abednego, Jonah and the 'whale' – and so we could go on. Here are tales which have captured the imagination of people across the centuries, and rightly so, for as well as communicating deep theological truths they also speak directly to our human condition. Time and again we can identify with the characters in question, seeing something of ourselves in each one. It is, perhaps, in the raw human emotions so often displayed and the almost brutal honesty before God that the Old Testament's greatest strength lies. So much of what we see there mirrors what we feel and experience ourselves.

Every individual will approach the complexities thrown up by the Old Testament in their own way. For me they reflect a nation's grappling with God across the centuries. From a crude awareness of God way back in the mists of time, we move inexorably forward to an ever-deepening understanding of his greatness, love and mercy, all brought together in the anticipation of the promised Messiah. Not that the coming of Jesus means our picture of God is complete, for we too must wrestle in our turn if we are to move forward in our journey of faith. God may be fully revealed in Christ, but for now we see only in part. Like his people of old, we must press on towards the kingdom he holds in store.

In this final volume we explore the message of the prophets, including among them, for convenience, Ezra and Nehemiah, although these do not strictly fit into that category. To sum up the message of even one of the lesser-known prophets in the space of a brief meditation is clearly an impossibility, let alone someone of the stature of Isaiah, Ezekiel or Jeremiah. This book, then, offers the briefest glimpse into the world of Old Testament prophecy, and no more. It attempts to give a flavour of each prophet's message while at the same time reminding us of the human face behind it. What led Obadiah and Nahum to gloat with almost vitriolic glee over the downfall of their neighbours? Why did Habakkuk puzzle over the purposes of God? How did Jeremiah feel when he first became aware of the call of God? These are just some of the questions these meditations explore.

Some of the prophets will be familiar to us. Who will not have heard at least something of the book of Isaiah – the unforgettable vision of chapter 6: 'In the year that King Uzziah died, I saw the Lord sitting on a throne' (verse 1), or the memorable picture of chapter 11: 'The wolf shall live with the lamb, the leopard shall lie down with the kid, the calf and the lion and the fatling together, and a little child shall lead them' (verse 6)? Other passages are similarly well known: Ezekiel's vision of the valley of dry bones, Jeremiah's picture of the potter moulding his clay, Jonah in the belly of the 'whale'; here, too, are haunting Old Testament images. But what of those like Haggai, Zephaniah or Malachi? How many are familiar with these books? How many have even read them? Yet each is part of the Scriptures, and each has a message for us. Not always an easy message, admittedly. At times we must dig deep beneath words which we find puzzling and even offensive, for there is much in these prophets which seems far-removed from the gospel. Yet if we are ready to persevere, God is able to speak to our own situation and our world today.

Each of the volumes in this collection is designed both for individual and group use. You may find them helpful in your personal devotions or equally they may provide material for a Bible study or house group. The themed 'chapters' have been set out with both ends in mind. They begin with an introductory paragraph which sets the scene for what follows. A scriptural reading then leads into a meditation, exploring the incidents related from the perspective of the principal character involved. The remaining sections are all designed to aid further reflec-tion. First, a selection of proverbs related to what has gone before is offered as food for thought. The relevance of some of these will be obvious, of others less so, but make time to consider their truth or otherwise. What does each one have to say about the subject under discussion? Do they aid understanding or confuse the issue? Do they sum up the key theme or point in an altogether different direction? This leads on to questions for discussion or personal reflection. There is no right or wrong answer to many of these questions; rather they are designed to help apply what the Bible has to say to our own lives. Don't rush through them with a cursory 'yes' or 'no'; ask yourself what each one is driving at and whether perhaps some have a challenge for you. Finally, additional passages of Scripture are recommended which may help you consider further the issues which have been raised; issues which are summed up in a concluding prayer.

Of course, it is impossible in a collection such as this to explore all the theological issues raised by the biblical passages referred to. My intention, instead, is to help the reader feel part of the incidents related and to draw out for themselves insights from these. Necessarily many questions will be left unanswered, but if anything in the pages which follow brings home the challenge of the Old Testament for today then I believe I will have been true to the overriding intention of all Scripture. It is my hope that through this collection of readings, prayers and meditations, familiar and not so familiar stories will come alive in new and unexpected ways.

Nick Fawcett

Opening prayer _____

Living God,
   there comes a time for us all
   when we must meet your challenge and respond –
   a time when, try as we might,
   we can no longer go on running from your presence.
The experience can be painful and disturbing –
   facing ourselves as we really are,
   looking into the darker recesses of our minds,
   and measuring all this against your infinite goodness.
We prefer to stifle the voice of conscience,
   to avoid the uncomfortable
   and deny what we would rather not accept,
   but until we make our peace with you
   we can find no rest for our souls.
Give us, then, the courage
   to wrestle with you in the wilderness
   until our doubts are resolved,
   our reservations overcome
   and our sins dealt with.
So may we experience for ourselves
   the blessings which you alone can give.
In the name of Christ.
Amen.

There is nothing patent in the New Testament
that is not latent in the Old.
(Anon)

1 The disturbing truth

Amos

One of the gifts I most admire is the ability to speak frankly, even when the truth may hurt. There are ways of doing this, of course – honesty always needs to be coupled with sensitivity – but the person we can depend on for a candid answer, come what may, is a priceless treasure indeed. Amos was such a person. The message God gave him to speak was not an easy one, and reception of it was bound to be hostile, especially as he was a prophet from Judah daring to poke his nose in the affairs of neighbouring Israel. Yet Amos knew that the words needed saying and he did not flinch from his call to be the bearer. I doubt many enjoyed what they heard, but those who were willing to take the message to heart and act upon it would have found the rewards more than worth it, for they would have re-established a meaningful relationship with the living God. What of us? Perhaps I'm wrong, but I suspect the challenge Amos brought is as much for you and me today as for those who initially heard it, for the problem he was addressing concerns the age-old dichotomy between religion and faith. To take the message of Amos seriously is a painful experience. Have we the courage to face it?

Reading – Amos 5:18-24

Alas for you who desire the day of the Lord!
Why do you want the day of the Lord?
It is darkness, not light;
as if someone fled from a lion,
and was met by a bear;
or went into the house and rested a hand against the wall,
and was bitten by a snake.
Is not the day of the Lord darkness, not light,
and gloom with no brightness in it?

I hate, I despise your festivals, and I take no delight in your solemn assemblies.
Even though you offer me your burnt offerings and grain offerings,
I will not accept them;
and the offerings of well-being of your fatted animals

I will not look upon.
Take away from me the noise of your songs;
I will not listen to the melody of your harps.
But let justice roll down like waters,
and righteousness like an everflowing stream.

Meditation

I thought I'd heard wrongly,
    my wires crossed somewhere,
    for the message was scandalous,
    too shocking even to contemplate, let alone proclaim.
Their sacrifices, meaningless?
Their worship, empty?
Their songs, noise?
Their offerings, worthless?
It seemed little short of blasphemy,
    a contradiction of everything I'd been taught since childhood,
    and for a moment my world was thrown into confusion.
Yet there was no getting away from it,
    that's what God was saying, loud and clear.
I struggled to take it in, you can imagine,
    wondering what on earth it could all mean,
    and wondering if I could dare proclaim it.
All right, so maybe they weren't Judeans,
    but then we can't all have everything, can we!
They were God's people, nonetheless,
    a devout nation just as we were,
    on the surface anyway –
    scrupulous in outward piety,
    meticulous in their attention to the Law,
    the sort of people you'd find it hard to find fault with,
    upright,
    godly,
    respectable,
    pillars of the local community.
So what was the problem?
How could God condemn them?
Only then I stopped,
    and looked not at their faith but their lives,
    not at their worship but their witness,
    and suddenly I saw it, clear as day.

It was all show –
>   their piety,
>   their zeal,
>   their rituals,
>   their prayers,
>   all just an empty facade belying a hollow interior.
They praised God,
>   but served self.
They preached justice,
>   but practised corruption.
Their words said one thing,
>   their deeds another.
And the tragedy is they couldn't see it,
>   eyes blinded by the trappings of religion,
>   outward observance everything,
>   substance replaced by shadow.
Those have their place, don't get me wrong,
>   but only as a means to an end,
>   never an end in themselves.
Forget that and there is nothing so sad,
>   and no one so lost;
>   for while you may think you have everything,
>   the reality is this:
>   you have nothing at all.

To ponder

- If you want to see black-hearted people, look among those who never miss their prayers. (*Chinese proverb*)
- A honey tongue, a heart of gall.
- All are not saints that go to church.
- Fine words dress ill deeds.
- Pretended holiness is double iniquity.
- The nearer the church, the farther from God.

To discuss

- In what ways can religion get in the way of Christianity? Can you think of examples, either from people you have met or from your own experience?

- Why do you think the people of Amos's day made the mistake they did? Can we fall into the same trap?
- Hypocrisy is one of the charges most frequently levelled against the Church. How justified is the accusation?

To consider further

Read James 2:14-17. Resolve to put your faith into practice in some concrete way this week. Reflect upon how far your words tally up with your actions.

Prayer

Lord,
 it's easy to go to church,
 hard to reach out to the world.
It's easy to say our prayers,
 hard to act upon them.
It's easy to offer our money,
 hard to give you our lives.
It's easy to sing your praises,
 hard to live to your glory.
Forgive us for so often taking the easy way;
 the way of outward show rather than inner faith.
Move within us,
 so that the words of our lips may show themselves
 in the thoughts of our hearts,
 and the claims of our faith be proven
 through the sincerity of our service.
Amen.

2 A love that will not let us go _____

_____ *Hosea*

One of the aspects of the Old Testament which puts many people off is the picture of God it sometimes portrays. In contrast to the portrait we see revealed in Christ, we see instead a stern and vengeful God, uncompromising in his anger and ready, where necessary, to punish without any apparent compunction. There can be no denying that such a portrayal of God is present, and we should beware of dismissing it too lightly, for we lose a sense of awe and reverence at our peril. Yet there is another portrait just as often painted, and nowhere is that more beautifully seen than in the book of the prophet Hosea. Taking as a model his own traumatic experience of a broken marriage, with all the heartbreak that must have entailed, he offers an insight into the anguish suffered by God at the repeated rejection and betrayal of his people. Here is an unforgettable glimpse into a love which refuses to let go despite everything that is thrown against it. There may be several pictures in the New Testament to rival it; there are few to better.

Reading – Hosea 11:1-9

When Israel was a child, I loved him,
and out of Egypt I called my son.
The more I called them,
the more they went from me;
they kept sacrificing to the Baals,
and offering incense to idols.

Yet it was I who taught Ephraim to walk,
I took them up in my arms;
but they did not know that I healed them.
I led them with cords of human kindness,
with bands of love.
I was to them like those
who lift infants to their cheeks.
I bent down to them and fed them.

They shall return to the land of Egypt,
and Assyria shall be their king,

because they have refused to return to me.
The sword rages in their cities,
it consumes their oracle-priests,
and devours because of their schemes.
My people are bent on turning away from me.
To the Most High they call,
but he does not raise them up at all.

How can I give you up, Ephraim?
How can I hand you over, O Israel?
How can I make you like Admah?
How can I treat you like Zeboiim?
My heart recoils within me;
my compassion grows warm and tender.
I will not execute my fierce anger;
I will not again destroy Ephraim;
for I am God and no mortal,
the Holy One in your midst,
and I will not come in wrath.

Meditation

I never realised how much he cared,
    how deeply and passionately he loved us.
He'd seemed remote up till then,
    set apart from us in splendid isolation,
    a God to approach with caution.
Not that I ever questioned his goodness –
    he'd been gracious to us from the beginning,
    calling us into being as a nation,
    delivering us time after time from oppression,
    leading us with infinite patience
    despite our refusal to follow –
    but I'd always had this picture of him as being distant,
    a God whose face we could never see,
    sovereign,
    righteous,
    holy,
    and ultimately, to be honest, a little frightening.
When we came to worship, we did so in awe,
    and as we knelt in prayer, we approached with trepidation,
    knowing he could judge as well as bless,
    punish, as well as save –

and let's face it, after the way we'd behaved
    there was every reason for punishment,
    and none at all for mercy.
We'd worshipped false gods,
    pale reflections of our own fears and fantasies,
    instead of the Lord of heaven and earth.
We'd oppressed the poor and exploited the weak,
    let greed run riot and vice go unchecked.
We'd said one thing and done another,
    spoken of justice yet practised deceit,
    so what reason had we to expect anything other than judgement,
    due recompense for all our sins?
Only he couldn't do it!
When the moment came to reach out and punish,
    he drew back,
    heart lurching within him –
    the memories too strong,
    his compassion too great,
    love refusing to be denied.
It wasn't any merit on our part which saved us,
    don't think that,
    no hidden virtue uncovered or past deed recalled.
We'd failed him completely,
    spurning his goodness and abusing his grace,
    yet, despite it all, he refused to let us go.
And I realised then that, despite his sovereignty
    and righteousness,
    still he loved us, more than we can ever begin to imagine;
    a love which will keep on giving,
    keep on burning
    and keep on reaching out for all eternity,
    whatever it may take,
    whatever it might cost!

To ponder

- God strikes with his finger, and not with all his arm.
- Love rules his kingdom without a sword.
- To err is human; to forgive, divine. *(Alexander Pope)*
- Love is not love which alters when it alteration finds. *(William Shakespeare)*

To discuss

- Are we guilty sometimes of limiting the extent of God's love, imagining that there is no way he can have time for us? What can cause us to think like this?

- Recall instances from your own life, or the experience of others, where love has refused to let go, despite being rejected repeatedly.

- Despite our good intentions, there are times when we knowingly hurt and betray those closest to us. What sort of things might lead to this? What leads us sometimes to turn our backs on the love of God?

To consider further

Read Luke 15:1-32 and 19:41-44. Give thanks for the wonderful love God has for all his people. Is God asking you to respond and, if so, in what way?

Prayer

Gracious God,
    we talk often about love,
    but we have little idea what it really is.
The love we show to others is invariably flawed,
    corrupted by ulterior motives and self-interest.
We can scarcely begin to fathom
    the immensity of the love you hold for us;
    a love that is inexhaustible,
    awesome in its intensity,
    devoted beyond measure.
Forgive us for losing sight
    of this one great reality at the heart of our faith
    without which all else is as nothing.
Forgive us for portraying you
    as a God of vengeance and justice
    when, above all, you are a God of love;
    a God who, despite our repeated disobedience,
    refuses to let us go.
Teach us to open our hearts to all you so freely give,
    and so may we love you and others
    with something of that same total commitment
    you unfailingly show.
In the name of Christ.
Amen.

3 The graciousness of God _____

_____ *Jonah*

Many of the characters in the Old Testament seem almost too good to be true. We can feel daunted by the depth of their piety, devotion and commitment. But not Jonah. One of the great appeals of this short book is the raw humanity of this reluctant prophet – a man with all the endearing qualities of our modern-day Victor Meldrew! Irascible, cold-hearted and petulant, he is just about the last person you would expect God to call into his service; his faults, if only he could see them, equally as great as the faults of those he was called to preach to. But that is the beauty of this story, for it vividly portrays God's amazing grace in action. No one in the narrative remotely deserves his blessing, yet all end up receiving it. The same holds true for us. We may pray 'forgive us our trespasses as we forgive those who trespass against us', but thankfully God is willing to go a good deal further than that. The consequences, if he wasn't, don't bear thinking about!

Reading – Jonah 1:1-3; 3:1-3a, 5; 3:10-4:4, 11

Now the word of the Lord came to Jonah son of Amittai, saying, 'Go at once to Nineveh, that great city, and cry out against it; for their wickedness has come up before me.' But Jonah set out to flee to Tarshish from the presence of the Lord. He went down to Joppa and found a ship going to Tarshish; so he paid his fare and went on board, to go with them to Tarshish, away from the presence of the Lord. . . .

The word of the Lord came to Jonah a second time, saying, 'Get up, go to Nineveh, that great city, and proclaim to it the message that I tell you.' So Jonah set out and went to Nineveh, according to the word of the Lord. . . . And the people of Nineveh believed God; they proclaimed a fast, and everyone, great and small, put on sackcloth.

When God saw what they did, how they turned from their evil ways, God changed his mind about the calamity that he had said he would bring upon them; and he did not do it. But this was very displeasing to Jonah, and he became angry. He prayed to the Lord and said, 'O Lord! Is this not what I said while I was still in my own country? That is why I fled to Tarshish at the beginning; for I knew that you are a gracious God and merciful, slow to anger, and abounding in steadfast love, and ready to relent from punishing. And now, O Lord, please take my life from me, for it is better for me to die than to live.' And the Lord said, 'Is it right for you to be angry? . . . Should I not be concerned about Nineveh, that great city, in which there are more than a hundred and twenty thousand persons who do not know their right hand from their left, and also many animals?'

Meditation

I knew it would happen, didn't I?
I knew those wretched Ninevites would go and repent
    if God gave them half a chance.
And that's precisely what they've done –
    covered themselves in sackcloth and ashes,
    grovelled in abject submission,
    and begged him for mercy.
Can't he see through them?
Apparently not,
    only too ready, it seems, to let bygones be bygones
    and embrace them with open arms.
Isn't that just typical of him,
    always ready to turn a blind eye
    the moment anyone claims to be sorry?
It's nauseating!
Honestly, can you blame me for running away like that
    the moment he called me?
I knew immediately what his game was –
    I've seen it happen all too often –
    this God of ours is too soft by half.
Why waste time pussy-footing around,
    that's what I'd like to know?
There were no excuses for Nineveh.
They must have known all along
    that what they were doing was wrong,
    the very name of the place synonymous with corruption,
    so why not just have done with it
    and wipe them off the face of the earth,
    put an end to it once and for all?
That's what I'd have done, and taken pleasure in it,
    but not God, oh no.
He has to send muggins, here, doesn't he,

to give them a warning,
knowing full well the moment they hear it
they'll be fawning on him like lovesick fools.
Oh yes, it's his right, I accept that –
if he reckons they're worth saving
then it's his business and no else's –
but why did he have to choose me? –
that's what I find hard to stomach.
He knows my feelings on the matter,
what I'd do to those Ninevites given half the chance,
so surely he could have chosen someone more suited to the task?
I can't understand him, I really can't;
you'd almost think he wants to teach me a lesson
as much as them.
Gracious me, what am I saying?
Whatever next!

To ponder

- God often visits us, but most of the time we are not at home. *(French proverb)*
- If there be any good in you, believe there is much more in others.
- The more a man knows, the more he forgives.
- If you wish your merits to be known, acknowledge those of other people. *(Oriental proverb)*
- Much of what we see depends on what we are looking for.

To discuss

- We do not know exactly how God spoke to Jonah, but it is clear that the prophet had a very clear sense of divine calling. Have we ever experienced such clarity of calling ourselves? In what ways are we typically aware of God speaking to us?
- What sort of things put us off from responding to God's call?
- Despite his rebellion, God dealt graciously and patiently with Jonah. Have we been aware of times when God has given us another chance to respond to his will?

To consider further

Read the story of Ananias in Acts 9:10-19, and of the two sons in Matthew 21:28-32. What parallels do we see in these with the story of Jonah, and what differences? Is there some avenue of service which God is calling you to but which you have been trying to ignore?

Prayer

Lord,
   it's easy to talk about loving others,
   much harder to mean it.
It's one thing to talk about forgiveness,
   quite another to put it into practice.
If we are honest,
   there are some people we find it hard to love
   and impossible to forgive.
We want people to suffer for the things they've done,
   to pay the price for their actions,
   and the thought of them getting off scot-free
   is one we find hard to accept.
Yet if you dealt with us according to our deserving,
   none of us could hope to escape punishment,
   for we have all failed you in ways too many to number.
Help us to recognise that your grace is greater
   than we can ever begin to imagine,
   and may we rejoice in the wonder of your love
   which embraces all.
Amen.

4 A clean sheet _____

_____ *Isaiah*

One of the tragedies of the Church is that it has acquired a reputation for being smug, self-righteous, holier than thou. How this has happened I do not know, for while some in the Church are more than ready to sit in judgement, by far the majority are all too aware of their own faults to point the accusing finger at others. Such, at least, has been my experience. The heart of the Christian message is one of forgiveness rather than judgement; about the God who is ready to accept us as we are, rather than as we should be. Of course, this involves a desire to change, but it begins and ends with God rather than ourselves. The truth of that may be most clearly demonstrated through Christ, but it was discovered centuries before by countless others. So it was that a young man, worshipping in the temple of Jerusalem, suddenly found himself faced by the call of God. Hopelessly inadequate though he felt, burdened by a profound sense of unworthiness, Isaiah discovered that God is always ready to take the initiative in breaking down the barriers which keep us from him.

Reading – Isaiah 6:1-8

In the year that King Uzziah died, I saw the Lord sitting on a throne, high and lofty; and the hem of his robe filled the temple. Seraphs were in attendance above him; each had six wings; with two they covered their faces, and with two they covered their feet, and with two they flew. And one called to another and said: 'Holy, holy, holy is the Lord of hosts; the whole earth is full of his glory.'

The pivots on the thresholds shook at the voices of those who called, and the house filled with smoke. And I said: 'Woe is me! I am lost, for I am a man of unclean lips, and I live among a people of unclean lips; yet my eyes have seen the King, the Lord of hosts!'

Then one of the seraphs flew to me, holding a live coal that had been taken from the altar with a pair of tongs. The seraph touched my mouth with it and said: 'Now that this has touched your lips, your guilt has departed and your sin is blotted out.' Then I heard the voice of the Lord saying, 'Whom shall I send, and who will go for us?' And I said, 'Here am I; send me!'

Meditation

Could it be true?
Could God, in his mercy, forgive even me?
It seemed incredible,
     too implausible for words,
     for there was so much in my life not as it should be,
     so many ways I daily let him down.
Does that surprise you,
     me being a prophet and all that?
It shouldn't do,
     for I was under no illusions as to my own importance,
     not for a moment.
If God ever wanted to use me
     it would be despite who I was, not because of it,
     that's what I'd always imagined.
My faults were all too apparent to me,
     and all too painful to contemplate.
I wanted to be different, don't get me wrong –
     there was nothing I'd have liked better
     than to offer faithful, unblemished service –
     but there was no escaping reality:
     I was as weak as the next man,
     unable to resist temptation,
     quick to go astray.
What reason was there to think I could change?
So when God appeared to me that day in the temple,
     I hate to say it, but I panicked,
     consumed by a sense of my own unworthiness.
It was only a vision, I know,
     but it brought home the shocking contrast
     between his purity and my sin,
     his strength and my weakness.
How could I ever bridge that gap?
There was no way I could even begin to,
     but the next moment I felt God reach out and touch me,
     summoning me to service,
     taking away my guilt,
     making me whole.
Me, Isaiah, a prophet?
Could it be true?
Could God really make me new?
It seemed beyond belief,
     childish, romantic nonsense!

Yet that's what he promised,
  and that's what he proved,
    not just to me but countless others across the years.
He called me to proclaim forgiveness,
  a new start for all,
    freedom from our sins.
And I've discovered, beyond all doubt,
    the wonderful, astonishing truth of that message –
    the simple, stupendous fact that whoever you are,
    whatever you've done,
    it doesn't matter;
    God is always ready to forgive what *has* been
    and take what *is*,
    shaping it by his grace to transform what's yet to be.

Reading – Isaiah 1:16-18

Wash yourselves; make yourselves clean; remove the evil of your doings from before my eyes; cease to do evil, learn to do good; seek justice, rescue the oppressed, defend the orphan, plead for the widow. Come now, let us argue it out, says the Lord; though your sins are like scarlet, they shall be white as snow; though they are red like crimson, they shall become like wool.

To ponder

- God forgives sins, otherwise heaven would be empty.
- God gives his wrath by weight, and without weight his mercy.
- He that sharply chides, is the most ready to pardon.
- Mercy surpasses justice.

To discuss

- Forgiving and forgetting is not as easy as it sounds, as many of us will know from experience. Do we really believe God forgives us in this way? If yes, do we live in such a way as to reflect this?
- What sort of things prevent us from accepting forgiveness from others? Do the same things stand in the way of accepting God's forgiveness? What is needed before we can be forgiven?

- What do we find hardest in forgiving others? What is the result of a failure to forgive on our part?

To consider further

Read Luke 5:1-11. Do we allow a sense of our unworthiness to stand in the way of our relationship with God? Learn from the experience of Peter, and recognise that in Christ we are accepted as we are, the slate wiped clean.

Prayer

Gracious God,
    we have no claim on your goodness,
      no reason to ever expect mercy.
Despite our best intentions, time and again we fail you,
      preferring our way to yours.
We say one thing, yet do another;
      we claim to love you, yet openly flout your will.
Forgive us, for, try as we might,
      we cannot seem to help ourselves.
Come to us, we pray,
      and blot out our faults.
Renew us through your Holy Spirit,
      redeem us through the grace of Christ,
      and remake us through your great love
      so that we may live and work for you,
      to the glory of your name.
Amen.

5 Vision of the future _____

_____ *Isaiah*

How would you feel if a politician or world leader were to promise a new and better world in which people everywhere will live in harmony; hatred, warfare and oppression a thing of the past; justice and freedom accorded to all? Would you believe it? I doubt it. We'd like to think it could be true, more than anything else, but I suspect most of us would take such claims with a strong pinch of salt. Life, we tell ourselves, is just not like that. Realism rather than idealism invariably wins the day. Such an attitude is understandable given the lamentable record of human history and the continuing divisions in our world today, yet it cannot finally be acceptable. *We* may abandon the world to its fate – *God* never will. He refuses to rest until that day when his will shall be done and his kingdom has come, on earth as it is in heaven. It may seem light years away from the world as we know it today, but we must never lose that vision of what life can become, nor stop working towards it.

Reading – Isaiah 11:1-9

A shoot shall come out from the stump of Jesse,
and a branch shall grow out of his roots.
The spirit of the Lord shall rest on him,
the spirit of wisdom and understanding,
the spirit of counsel and might,
the spirit of knowledge and the fear of the Lord.
His delight shall be in the fear of the Lord.

He shall not judge by what his eyes see,
or decide by what his ears hear;
but with righteousness he shall judge the poor
and decide with equity for the meek of the earth;
he shall strike the earth with the rod of his mouth,
and with the breath of his lips he shall kill the wicked.
Righteousness shall be the belt around his waist,
and faithfulness the belt around his loins.

The wolf shall live with the lamb,
the leopard shall lie down with the kid,
the calf and the lion and the fatling together,
and a little child shall lead them.
The cow and the bear shall graze,
their young shall lie down together;
and the lion shall eat straw like the ox.
The nursing child shall play over the hole of the asp,
and the weaned child shall put its hand on the adder's den.
They will not hurt or destroy on all my holy mountain;
for the earth will be full of the knowledge of the Lord
as the waters cover the sea.

Meditation

Does this sound daft to you –
    a wolf living with a lamb,
    a lion grazing with an ox,
    a child playing happily with a snake?
It does to me, I have to admit it,
    now that I've had time to consider the implications.
But it didn't at the time,
    not when the idea first caught hold of me.
You see, I had this picture of a different kind of world,
    a society where barriers are broken down,
      where all the petty disputes that so often divide us
      are a thing of the past.
Imagine it –
    no more violence,
    no more fear,
    no more hatred,
    no more suffering;
    a world at one with itself,
    all creatures living together in harmony,
    nation existing peaceably alongside nation,
    people set free to be themselves –
    valued,
    loved,
    respected,
    not for what we can get out of them,
    but simply for what they are.
Is that so daft?

Well yes, it probably is,
   because nine times out of ten,
   ninety-nine times out of a hundred,
   for most of us, when the pressure's on,
   it's number one who comes first,
   a question of 'I'm all right and never mind the rest'.
We'd like it to be different, obviously,
   but even when we're not simply paying lip-service to high ideals,
   we can't finally change ourselves, try as we might.
Yet give me one thing –
   it's a wonderful idea, isn't it,
   this world of peace and justice? –
   a beautiful picture –
   worth striving for, I'd say,
   even worth dying for.
And who knows, one day,
   just maybe,
   somebody might actually come along
   with the faith and courage not just to dream about it,
   but to bring it about;
   not simply to share the vision,
   but to live in such a way that it becomes real –
   God's kingdom, here on earth.

To ponder

- Where there is peace, God is.
- Love is heaven, and heaven is love. *(Sir Walter Scott)*
- Heaven lies about us in our infancy! *(William Wordsworth)*
- Thou hast said much here of 'Paradise Lost' but what hast thou to say of 'Paradise Found'? *(Ellwood Thomas)*

To discuss

- Isaiah looks forward to a new era of world harmony; a time when all will live in peace. Must this vision be reserved for the kingdom of heaven, or is it one we should hope to build, at least in part, in the world here and now?
- Is there a danger sometimes of us becoming so preoccupied with

spiritual matters that we neglect our responsibilities to the world?
Can we be so heavenly minded as to be of no earthly use?

• What practical steps can we take to promote peace and reconciliation?

To consider further

Read Revelation 7:9-17. What similarities are there between the vision
of John and the vision of Isaiah? What differences are there? Which
speaks to you most?

Prayer

Gracious God,
    sometimes we look at this world of ours
    and we despair.
We see its greed, corruption, hatred and violence,
    and we ask, 'How can it ever change?'
The heady dreams of youth are worn down
    on the treadmill of experience
    until a world-weary cynicism takes over.
Although we still make the right noises,
    in our hearts we have given up expecting any real change.
Forgive us that sense of despair, Lord.
Forgive us for losing sight of all you are able to do.
Move within us rekindling faith and hope,
    and so help us not just to believe change can happen
    but to play our part in ensuring it does.
Amen.

6 From small beginnings _____

_____ *Micah*

It's always pleasing, isn't it, when a midget turns the tables on a giant? Whether it is a non-league football team defeating their premier league relations, a village store fighting off competition from an out-of-town supermarket, or a local pressure group resisting the plans of a multi-national company, our hearts warm to tales of the underdog come good. Partly it's because we enjoy seeing the powerful and influential brought down a peg or two, but more important is the conviction such stories give us that unpromising beginnings need not be a barrier to success. This is a theme which runs throughout the pages of the Old Testament – from Moses taking on the might of Egypt to David killing Goliath, from Elijah triumphing over the prophets of Baal to Daniel facing up to the terrors of the lions' den. The prophet Micah adds one more unforgettable picture to the list in the little town of Bethlehem so beloved of Christmas carols. It is hard today to appreciate how extraordinary it must have seemed at the time to hear God's promised Messiah associated with this insignificant and out-of-the-way town, notwithstanding its associations with King David. Jerusalem, surely, was the natural choice for such a ruler – the only place fitting for someone of such stature! In human terms, this may have been true, but not in God's. As so often before and since, God proves himself to be a God of the unexpected. In his kingdom the first invariably find themselves last, and the last first.

Reading – Micah 5:2-5a

But you, O Bethlehem of Ephrathah,
who are one of the little clans of Judah,
from you shall come forth for me
one who is to rule in Israel,
whose origin is from of old, from ancient days.
Therefore he shall give them up until the time
when she who is in labour has brought forth;
then the rest of his kindred shall return
to the people of Israel.
And he shall stand and feed his flock in the strength of the Lord,

in the majesty of the name of the Lord his God.
And they shall live secure, for now he shall be great
to the ends of the earth;
and he shall be the one of peace.

Meditation

Bethlehem – not much of a place, is it?
I can't pretend otherwise.
Nothing special about it, or unusual,
    just your typical Judean town really,
    a sleepy provincial backwater
    quietly going about its own business.
And why not?
Don't think I'm knocking it –
    quite the opposite –
    it just isn't the sort of place you'd expect
    to hit the headlines,
    still less to set the world on fire.
Yet you know what,
    ever since I passed through last week
    I've had this strange feeling
    that God has put his finger on that town,
    singled it out for a particular purpose,
    a special honour that will give it a place in history for ever.
Yes, ridiculous, I know –
    I've told myself that time and time again these last few days –
    but it makes no difference,
    I just can't get the idea out of my head.
It's raised a few eyebrows, I can tell you –
    a right one we've got here,
    that's what people are thinking when I tell them.
And who can blame them?
'Prove it!' they tell me.
'Show us the evidence!'
And of course I can't, for there isn't any;
    just this hunch that God was speaking to me.
Yet before you write the idea off completely,
    stop and think for a minute,
    for is it really as way out as it first sounds?
Wouldn't it actually be typical of the way God so often works –
    confounding our expectations,
    turning our view of the world upside down,

using the little to accomplish the great,
the insignificant to achieve the spectacular,
the humble to astonish the proud?
Remember Moses! Joshua! David!
Remember Egypt! Jericho! Goliath!
Time and again it's been the same story –
where God is concerned, small is beautiful.
I may, of course, be wrong this time, I accept that.
It could simply be some crazy bee in my bonnet.
But I don't think so.
In fact the more I think about it
the more certain I feel it's the way God will choose –
surprising us not simply through his coming
but through the very way he comes.
You may think different, it's up to you –
keep on looking to Jerusalem if you want to.
But me?
I'm looking to Bethlehem,
the last place you'd expect, admittedly,
but in God's eyes, last but not least!

To ponder

- Everything has its seed.
- Rivers need a spring.
- Every oak must first be an acorn.
- Everything must have a beginning.
- From a little spark may burst a mighty flame. *(Dante)*
- The beginnings of all things are small. *(Cicero)*

To discuss

- Are there times when you have surprised yourself by achieving something you thought yourself incapable of? Have others surprised you in a similar way?
- Recall incidents when seeming 'Davids' have overcome 'Goliaths'. What do you think was the key to their success? Can we learn anything from their example?
- Are we guilty even in the Church sometimes of judging strength and success by outside appearances? Is the size of a church and its number of converts a reliable measure of its effectiveness?

To consider further

Read Mark 4:30-32 and Luke 17:5-6. Remind yourself how God is able to use what we consider insignificant, and resolve to step out in faith this week, even though that step may be very small. Stop underestimating what God can do through you!

Prayer

Sovereign God,
    time and again you have overturned human expectations,
    using the most unlikely of people
    in yet more unlikely surroundings.
You have shown beyond doubt that no situation or person
    is outside the scope of your purpose –
    that each one can be used by you.
Teach us, then, to be open
    to everything you would do through those around us,
    and to recognise also all you can do through us,
    working in ways we would never dare to contemplate
    and can scarcely imagine.
Sovereign God,
    you recognise the potential of everyone and everything –
    help us to do the same.
Amen.

7 Rough justice?

Nahum

The book of Nahum has much in common with that of Obadiah, its theme one of undisguised glee at a catastrophe about to befall the enemies of Judah. The parallel goes further, for all this is interpreted by the prophet as proof that, despite appearances to the contrary, God will ensure that justice is finally done. That must have taken some believing, since for generations the people of Judah had suffered under the yoke of the mighty Assyrian empire. Yet sure enough, within a few years this seemingly impregnable dynasty was to collapse, as a new super-power, Babylon, emerged to take centre stage in the ancient world. In recent years we have seen events just as remarkable in the destruction of the Berlin Wall, the end of the Cold War, the removal of apartheid, and the successive overthrow of dictatorial regimes the world over. All this is not to say that everything in this life works out as it should, for there are times when it manifestly does not. Yet at the heart of our faith is the conviction that God is actively involved in human history, striving to establish his kingdom despite everything which conspires to frustrate his purpose.

Reading – Nahum 1:2-10

A jealous and avenging God is the Lord,
the Lord is avenging and wrathful;
the Lord takes vengeance on his adversaries
and rages against his enemies.
The Lord is slow to anger but great in power,
and the Lord will by no means clear the guilty.

His way is in whirlwind and storm,
and the clouds are the dust of his feet.
He rebukes the sea and makes it dry,
and he dries up all the rivers;
Bashan and Carmel wither,
and the bloom of Lebanon fades.
The mountains quake before him,
and the hills melt;
the earth heaves before him,
the world and all who live in it.

Who can stand before his indignation?
Who can endure the heat of his anger?
His wrath is poured out like fire,
and by him the rocks are broken in pieces.
The Lord is good,
a stronghold in a day of trouble;
he protects those who take refuge in him,
even in a rushing flood.
He will make a full end of his adversaries,
and will pursue his enemies into darkness.
Why do you plot against the Lord?
He will make an end;
no adversary will rise up twice.
Like thorns they are entangled,
like drunkards they are drunk;
they are consumed like dry straw.

Meditation

Do you ever stop and wonder about the fairness of life?
I do, or at least I used to.
It's hard not to, isn't it,
    when all around you see evil going unpunished
    and good trampled underfoot?
And for years that's precisely what we *did* see,
    a regime as corrupt and cruel
    as any you might care to imagine,
    greed, envy, wickedness rampant within it,
    rotten to the core.
We'd suffered it all as best we could,
    but faith had worn thin and hope run dry.
'Where was God?' we couldn't help asking.
'How could he sit back and allow an empire like that to hold sway,
    lording it over the nations?
It made a nonsense of everything –
    our convictions,
    our teaching,
    our faith in God's eternal purpose –
    everything ultimately called into question.
It was impossible not to doubt,
    and there were many all too willing to voice their feelings,
    such was their anger and frustration

at the seeming injustice of it all.
I was the same for a time,
 as confused and bitter as any;
 but not any more,
 for suddenly the tables have been turned,
 the boot now firmly on the other foot,
 and with it my faith has been restored.
It's wrong to gloat, I know,
 but wouldn't you feel the same
 if you'd been through what we faced –
 your land pillaged,
 your people humiliated,
 your God usurped by worthless idols?
We'd had no choice but to listen to their jibes,
 pander to their wishes,
 but now it's different –
 at long last they must reap what they've sown,
 stand up and give account for their crimes,
 and you won't catch me shedding any tears.
Let them pay, that's what I say,
 no sentence too harsh,
 no punishment too severe.
You think me heartless?
You're probably right.
But it's good at last to see evil conquered and truth prevail,
 to see hatred and violence put in their place,
 pride heading for a fall.
I'm not saying it answers everything, not by a long way,
 for there'll be others to step into their shoes just as evil;
 yet I know now, with a certainty nothing can destroy,
 whatever we may face,
 however hopeless it may seem,
 God's will shall triumph
 and right will prevail!

To ponder

- God comes with leaden feet, but strikes with iron hands.
- God stays long, but strikes at last.
- God is a sure paymaster.
- Life must be lived forwards, but can only be understood backwards.
  (Sören Kierkegaard)

To discuss

- What apparent injustices in life trouble you most? Discuss these openly and honestly.
- Have there been particular moments in your life which have restored your faith in the purposes of God? What were they?

To consider further

Read 2 Thessalonians 2:1-12. What do you make of this picture of judgement? Can there finally be a place for everyone in God's kingdom?

Prayer

Lord,
   we can't help wondering sometimes what life is all about.
When we see the good suffer and the wicked prosper
      our faith is shaken,
      and we inevitably start to question.
There is so much we cannot understand,
      so much that seems to contradict
      everything we believe about you.
Teach us that, despite all this, you are there,
      striving against everything which frustrates your will
      and denies your love.
Teach us to hold on to those moments in life
      when we see wrongs righted and justice done at last.
Above all, teach us to look at the cross of Christ,
      and to draw strength from the victory of love
      over what had seemed to be the triumph of evil.
Amen.

8 A day of reckoning

Zephaniah

The older one gets, the more one comes to recognise that life isn't fair. The heady idealism of youth gives way to the hard-headed realism of middle age, as the truth slowly dawns that, in this life at least, people don't always get what they deserve. Honesty may be the best policy when it comes to peace of mind, but it is not necessarily the most lucrative. The unpleasant truth is that all too often cheats *do* prosper. Coming to terms with facts like this is a painful business and one which can test faith to the limit, just as it did in the time of Zephaniah. There were many in his day who, faced by the apparent injustices of life, concluded that God was either disinterested in human affairs or power-less to intervene. It was an understandable mistake, but one which the prophet had no time for. In God's time, he warns, justice will be done, and be seen to be done by all. We lose sight of that at our peril.

Reading – Zephaniah 1:7a, 10-16; 3:9-13

Be silent before the Lord God!
For the day of the Lord is at hand.

On that day, says the Lord,
a cry will be heard from the Fish Gate,
a wail from the Second Quarter,
a loud crash from the hills.
The inhabitants of the Mortar wail,
for all the traders have perished;
all who weigh out silver are cut off.
At that time I will search Jerusalem with lamps,
and I will punish the people
who rest complacently on their dregs,
those who say in their hearts,
'The Lord will not do good, nor will he do harm.'
Their wealth shall be plundered,
and their houses laid waste.
Though they shall build houses,
they shall not inhabit them;
though they plant vineyards,
they shall not drink wine from them.

The great day of the Lord is near,
near and hastening fast;
the sound of the day of the Lord is bitter,
the warrior cries aloud there.
That day will be a day of wrath,
a day of distress and anguish,
a day of ruin and devastation,
a day of clouds and thick darkness,
a day of trumpet blast and battle cry
against the fortified cities
and against the lofty battlements.

At that time I will change the speech of the peoples
to a pure speech,
that all of them may call on the name of the Lord
and serve him with one accord.
From beyond the rivers of Ethiopia
my suppliants, my scattered ones,
shall bring my offering.
On that day you shall not be put to shame
because of all the deeds by which you have rebelled against me;
for then I will remove from your midst
your proudly exultant ones,
and you shall no longer be haughty
in my holy mountain.
For I will leave in the midst of you
a people humble and lowly.
They shall seek refuge in the name of the Lord –
the remnant of Israel;
they shall do no wrong and utter no lies,
nor shall a deceitful tongue
be found in their mouths.
Then they will pasture and lie down,
and no one shall make them afraid.

Meditation

'Does it matter?' they said.
'Does it make a scrap of difference –
   the way we act,
   the way we think –
   to the course our lives will take?'

They'd believed so once, no question,
    each one of them convinced that one step out of line
    and God would be down on them
    like a ton of bricks,
    a rod of iron,
    swift to exact revenge.
A God of justice, that's how they'd seen him,
    rewarding good and punishing evil.
But that was then,
    and this is now.
They'd seen the way of the world since then –
    how the strong crush the weak and the rich fleece the poor,
    how virtue goes unrewarded and evil seems to thrive.
'What had God done to stop it?' they wanted to know.
'When had he ever stepped in
    to tip the scales and set things right?'
Well, if he had, it wasn't in their lifetime –
    the theory said one thing,
    the facts said another –
    so look to yourself, they told me,
    for no one else will:
    not God,
    not man,
    not anyone.
Is that how you see it?
I hope not,
    for they couldn't be more wrong.
There may not be a thunderbolt from on high,
    instant punishment to fit the crime,
    but did anyone say there would be? –
    if that's how God works then heaven help the lot of us.
Yet if they really believe he doesn't care,
    that he's twiddling his thumbs in divine indifference,
    they're in for a rude awakening.
Perhaps not today,
    perhaps not tomorrow,
    but the reckoning *will* come –
    a time when each will reap what they have sown,
    finally called to account for their actions.
Make no mistake, it will happen,
    corruption caught at last in its own web,
    evil poisoned by its own venom,
    and when it does all flesh will know that he is God,

sovereign in judgement,
  ruler over all.
Ignore me if you like,
  it's up to you –
  it's your future we're talking about,
  you who must face the consequences.
Only remember this:
  when the party's over and the inquest begins,
  when the court sits and the verdict is given,
  don't say I didn't warn you.

To ponder

- Crime doesn't pay.
- Punishment is lame, but it comes.
- He that steals honey should beware of the sting.
- Ill-gotten goods never prosper.
- He that does what he should not, shall feel what he would not.

To discuss

- Is there a sense in which wrong-doing carries its own punishment? Is it true that crime doesn't pay? In what way?
- Would it make any difference to the way you live and act if you knew you could do something wrong and get away with it?
- Since God is ready to forgive us when we make mistakes, there's no need to worry too much about stepping out of line. What's wrong with this line of reasoning?

To consider further

Read Hebrews 10:23-39. Are there areas in our faith or morality where we have become casual, bending the rules so often that we no longer even notice? Do we take God's judgement as well as his mercy seriously? Take a long hard look at yourself and resolve to change where necessary.

Prayer

Sovereign God,
    we cannot help wondering sometimes
    about the justice of life.
We see so much that is wrong,
    so much we cannot make sense of,
    and we ask ourselves why you stand by and let it happen.
Day after day we watch helplessly
    as truth is trodden underfoot,
    love exploited,
    and the innocent suffer,
    while those who least deserve it seem to flourish.
Help us, confronted by such enigmas, not to lose heart.
Teach us to recognise that loving you brings its own rewards,
    greater than any this world can offer,
    and remind us also that the time will come
    when everyone will answer to you,
    and justice will prevail.
Amen.

Ken
2/06

9 Life's riddle _____

Habakkuk

I like the book of Habakkuk. There's something hugely refreshing about the honesty with which it tackles the enigmas of life. No pious acceptance here that all which happens must somehow be God's will. No tortuous attempt to find a spiritual explanation for everything. For this prophet the world presents deep puzzles, puzzles for which he seeks some answers. Those who find his questions disturbing may prefer to gloss over them, turning instead to the less controversial passages which follow, but to do that is to bury one's head in the sand. Avoiding the issues helps no one, for the challenge does not go away. Simplistic answers are equally unhelpful, and in the long run do more harm than good. Personally, I believe God prefers an honest cry of confusion to a faith which deals with life's riddles by sweeping them under the carpet.

Reading – Habakkuk 1:2-4

O Lord, how long shall I cry for help,
and you will not listen?
Or cry to you, 'Violence!'
and you will not save?
Why do you make me see wrongdoing
and look at trouble?
Destruction and violence are before me;
strife and contention arise.
So the law becomes slack
and justice never prevails.
The wicked surround the righteous –
therefore judgement comes forth perverted.

Meditation

What's going on?
Can anyone tell me?
I thought this God of ours was meant to be good,
   on the side of justice, love, righteousness;

a God who rewards the faithful and punishes the wicked.
Well, it's a nice thought,
   but you could have fooled me!
I look around and see just the opposite,
   greed, hatred, violence everywhere;
   corruption carrying off the spoils
   while the weak go to the wall.
It's the law of the jungle out there,
   every man for himself,
   and it seems to me God is doing nothing about it,
   turning a blind eye to the whole sorry business.
I'm sorry if that shocks you,
   but that's the way it feels sometimes,
   and I'm fed up pretending otherwise.
Oh, the time will come when the tables are turned,
   don't misunderstand me;
   one day we'll see right prevail and love emerge victorious –
   I hold on to that conviction with all my being,
   the one thing that makes sense of this mystifying world of ours.
But don't tell me it works like that here and now,
   that the good will prosper,
   the upright be vindicated,
   for quite clearly it isn't so.
I've watched the innocent suffer, the blameless abused.
I've seen the weak exploited, the poor crushed.
I've witnessed naked greed,
   wanton desire,
   brazen deceit,
   each vying for power,
   and each achieving their ends.
Don't think I doubt God,
   I don't,
   but I question the way we dress him up,
   and I question a faith which claims sin brings suffering
   and obedience reward,
   for it's just not that simple,
   not that simple at all.
It's up to you, of course,
   you may disagree,
   call me a heretic,
   a blasphemer –
   it's your right.
But next time life rears up and bites you,

ask yourself this:
is it God's doing? –
his wrath? –
his punishment? –
or is he suffering there with you,
sharing your anger,
voicing your pain,
and longing for that day
when not just *your* questions, but *his*,
will finally receive their answer?

Reading – Habakkuk 3:17-19

Though the fig tree does not blossom,
and no fruit is on the vines;
though the produce of the olives fails,
and the fields yield no food;
though the flock is cut off from the fold,
and there is no herd in the stalls,
yet I will rejoice in the Lord;
I will exult in the God of my salvation.
God, the Lord, is my strength;
he makes my feet like the feet of a deer,
and makes me tread upon the heights.

To ponder

- He that nothing questions, nothing learns.
- The more one knows, the less one believes.
- Doubt is the key of knowledge. *(Persian proverb)*
- He that knows nothing, doubts nothing.

To discuss

- Do you believe there's a place for doubt in the Christian life? Is it a strength or a weakness? Why? Is asking questions a sign of faith or disbelief?
- Are you open to the possibility of deeply held convictions being challenged? Can faith grow if it is not first stretched?

To consider further

Read Mark 9:24. Openly acknowledge before God the things you don't understand, and ask for help and courage to wrestle with them honestly.

Prayer

Lord,
    we can't make sense of life sometimes,
    and it is foolish even to try,
    for we know that this world is not as you want it to be.
We pray day by day,
    'Your kingdom come, your will be done',
    and in that prayer we recognise
    that your purpose is constantly being frustrated,
    your will repeatedly blocked.
Save us, then, when life is a mystery,
    from blaming you.
Deliver us from a naïve faith
    which assumes that if we follow you
    material blessing and worldly satisfaction will surely follow.
Help us, despite everything which conspires against you,
    to hold on to the conviction
    that in the fullness of time
    good will conquer evil,
    and your love triumph over all.
Amen.

10 The unwelcome call

Jeremiah

Wouldn't it be wonderful if God spoke to us in a clear and unmistakable way? Have you ever thought that? I have. But how would we feel if it actually happened? Would God's call be as welcome as we like to think? The experience of Jeremiah suggests it might be anything but. There was no doubting the call when it came, but, in a way reminiscent of Moses long before him, Jeremiah did his level best to resist what God was asking. 'I'm too young,' he retorted, 'too raw, too inexperienced.' No doubt he had a point, yet, reading between the lines, it is clear that the soon-to-be-prophet did not relish the task put to him. It was an ambivalence which was to remain with him throughout his ministry. And in that formative encounter is a powerful reminder that the call of God isn't always the easy thing we might imagine. On the contrary, it can demand of us more than we feel able to give, bringing joy, undoubtedly, but potentially sorrow in equal measure. All we can say with assurance is that whatever God asks us to do he will give us the strength to complete, not finally through any special qualities on our part, although God may well use these, but through his sheer grace which, in the celebrated words of the Apostle Paul, 'is able to accomplish abundantly far more than all we can ask or imagine'.

Reading – Jeremiah 1:4-10; 20:7-9

Now the word of the Lord came to me saying, 'Before I formed you in the womb I knew you, and before you were born I consecrated you; I appointed you a prophet to the nations.' Then I said, 'Ah, Lord God! Truly I do not know how to speak, for I am only a boy.' But the Lord said to me, 'Do not say, "I am only a boy"; for you shall go to all whom I send you, and you shall speak whatever I command you. Do not be afraid of them, for I am with you to deliver you, says the Lord.' Then the Lord put out his hand and touched my mouth; and the Lord said to me, 'Now I have put my words in your mouth. See, today I appoint you over nations and over kingdoms, to pluck up and to pull down, to destroy and to overthrow, to build and to plant.'

(The fears expressed by Jeremiah in the above passage from Chapter 1 are shown, in the following verses from Chapter 20, to have been well founded, but so also is God's promise to put his words in Jeremiah's mouth.)

Lord, you have enticed me,
and I was enticed;
you have overpowered me,
and you have prevailed.
I have become a laughingstock all day long;
everyone mocks me.
For whenever I speak, I must cry out,
I must shout, 'Violence and destruction!'
For the word of the Lord has become for me
a reproach and derision all day long.
If I say, 'I will not mention him,
or speak any more in his name,'
then within me there is something like burning fire
shut up in my bones;
I am weary of holding it in,
and I cannot.

Meditation

It was the last thing I expected,
    the last thing I wanted –
    me, Jeremiah, a prophet?
Ridiculous!
I was just a boy,
    still learning the ways of the world,
    no experience of life at all,
    the very idea of speaking in public purgatory to me.
So I told him straight:
    'Sorry, Lord, but no thank you.
    Ask someone else, not me!'
Blunt perhaps,
    but there was no point beating around the bush, was there?
I knew my strengths and limitations, as well as anyone,
    and this was beyond me, I had no doubt of it.
Only he wouldn't take no for an answer.
Don't look at yourself, he said,
    look at me!
It's not *your* gifts, *your* wisdom, *your* words that matter,
    but *mine*,
    and you can rest assured that I will be with you
    whenever you need me,

ready to speak,
ready to strengthen,
ready to save.
What could I say?
There was no escape.
I suppose I could have argued,
but I wasn't rebellious by nature
and if God thought he could use me, fine –
only I honestly didn't think he could.
There were so many others more gifted than me,
more qualified for the job;
teachers, preachers, leaders,
each one of them naturals,
capable of captivating the crowds with their gift of oratory,
holding them spellbound through their subtle way with words.
Me? – I went weak at the knees at the very thought.
Yet God, apparently, could see something in me I couldn't,
qualities I never knew existed,
and he's used them since then in a way that has left me staggered.
No, I can't say I've enjoyed being a prophet,
quite the contrary –
it's been costly,
demanding,
and at times downright dangerous,
precious few welcoming the message I've brought,
and plenty being positively hostile.
But the words had to be spoken,
the message delivered,
and despite the way I sometimes felt,
I was the one to do it,
no way I could keep silent,
much though I often longed to.
Call me mad if you like –
plenty have –
but I haven't finished yet, not by a long way,
and I don't think I ever will,
for it's my countrymen we're talking about here,
foolish, stubborn, sinful perhaps,
yet still my people and still God's,
so as long as there's the chance of even one person listening,
one person's life being turned around,
I'll go on proclaiming the message
until I draw my final breath.

To ponder

- God makes the back for the burden.
- Since God has not bent the top of the palm-tree, he has given a long neck to the giraffe. *(Arabic proverb)*
- For a web begun, God sends the thread.
- God tempers the wind to the shorn lamb.

To discuss

- Have there been times when you have resisted what you believe to be God's calling? Why?
- Have there been occasions in your life when you have achieved things you felt beyond you? What was the secret behind your success?
- Does the Church today lay too much emphasis upon the rewards of discipleship and not enough on the cost?

To consider further

Read 1 Corinthians 1:26-31 and Galatians 1:10-24. Do you underestimate the way God is able to use you? Is it time you responded to his call?

Prayer

Lord God,
 there are times when we wish you'd never called us
 to discipleship.
When the demands made upon us are too many
 and the cost seems too great,
 when you ask of us more than we feel capable of,
 we can't help wondering if we've made a mistake
 in committing ourselves to your service.
Yet you see in us gifts
 which we have not even begun to recognise,
 and you are able to supply what is lacking
 to use us in ways we would never dream possible.
Teach us then to look at life with your eyes,
 seeing not the obstacles but the possibilities,
 and so may we respond in faith,
 offering our all to you
 in confident expectation and joyful praise.
Amen.

11 Keeping faith

Jeremiah

Perhaps one of the greatest dangers we can face in the Christian life is cynicism. We start off on the road of discipleship full of enthusiasm, believing life has really changed and that from then on it will be different, but as the years pass, and time and again we find the old self rearing its ugly head, so we begin to wonder if the transformation effected by Christ is as real as we thought. No matter how hard we try, we cannot seem to rid ourselves of our basic human failings, despite God's promise to make us new. Such frustrations would, I suspect, have sounded a chord with the prophet Jeremiah, called as he was to preach repentance and subsequent renewal to the people of Judah. How many, I wonder, shrugged their shoulders indifferently when they heard his message. It sounded good, but experience had taught them that they would go on making the same mistakes in the future just as they had in the past. Jeremiah believed different, looking forward to the day when God would establish a new covenant with his people, transforming them from within. It is a covenant, of course, which has been made through the death and resurrection of Christ, but, though the work of renewal has begun, its fulfilment awaits that day when he shall return in glory to draw all things to himself. Never lose sight of that promise: what he has done and what he has yet to do.

Reading – Jeremiah 31:31-34

The days are surely coming, says the Lord, when I will make a new covenant with the house of Israel and the house of Judah. It will not be like the covenant that I made with their ancestors when I took them by the hand to bring them out of the land of Egypt – a covenant that they broke, though I was their husband, says the Lord. But this is the covenant that I will make with the house of Israel after those days, says the Lord: I will put my law within them, and I will write it on their hearts; and I will be their God, and they shall be my people. No longer shall they teach one another, or say to each other, 'Know the Lord,' for they shall all know me, from the least of them to the greatest, says the Lord; for I will forgive their iniquity, and remember their sin no more.

Meditation

You're wasting your time, they tell me,
    chasing an impossible dream –
    one they'd like to believe in, could it possibly come true,
    but hopelessly unrealistic,
    naïve to the point of folly.
And to be honest, I can't say I blame them,
    for when you look at our record,
    our history as a nation,
    there seems as much chance of us mending our ways
    as a leopard changing its spots.
We've tried to be different, heaven knows,
    striven body and soul to turn over a new leaf,
    but somehow we always end up
    making the same mistakes we've always made,
    the spirit willing but the flesh weak.
So, yes, when they hear me speaking of new beginnings,
    a fresh start,
    it's hardly surprising they nod their heads knowingly
    with a wry smile and surreptitious wink.
They've seen it all before, too many times –
    promises made only to be broken,
    good intentions flourishing for a moment
    only to come to nothing –
    what reason to think it should be any different now?
Yet it can be, I'm sure of it,
    not because of anything *we* might do
    but because of what *God* will do for us,
    working within,
    moulding,
    shaping,
    like a potter fashioning his clay,
    until his love flows through our hearts
    and his grace floods our whole being.
It sounds far-fetched, I know,
    a wild and foolish fantasy,
    and whether I'll see it in my lifetime, who can say?
But I honestly believe that one day the time will come –
    a day when God breaks down the barriers which keep us apart,
    when through his great mercy we become a new creation,
    healed,
    restored,
    forgiven –

and in that hope I will continue to serve him,
speaking the word he has given,
confident that in the fullness of time it shall be fulfilled!

To ponder

- Have at it, and have it.
- Step after step and the ladder is ascended.
- Little strokes fell great oaks.
- Never say die.
- Seek till you find, and you'll not lose your labour.

To discuss

- How often have you made New Year or Lenten resolutions which have come to nothing? Do you still set yourselves goals such as these, or have you given up all hope of ever changing?
- Why do we find it so hard to kick old habits? Is it possible for someone to have their life turned around, or is it true that 'a leopard cannot change its spots'?
- What reassurance would you offer to someone who has become disillusioned about themselves and the power of anything to make a difference to their lives?

To consider further

Read Hebrews 11:32-12:3. Stop dwelling on your own failures and focus instead on the example of Jesus.

Prayer

Gracious God,
    you know how much we want to serve you.
We have resolved so many times
    to live more faithfully as your people
    that we have lost count,

yet, somehow, when the moment of challenge comes
    we are found wanting.
Despite the good which we long to do,
    we fall victim yet again to the same old weaknesses,
    unable to conquer the feebleness of our sinful nature.
Have mercy, O God,
    and renew us through your Holy Spirit.
Cleanse us through the love of Christ,
    and put a new heart and a right spirit within us.
Dwell within us and fill our souls
    so that truly you may be our God
    and we shall be your people.
Amen.

12 A glimpse of glory

Ezekiel

The more established we become in our faith, the more fixed our picture of God tends to become. It's not that we consciously let this happen; rather it is the old story of settling into a rut as the years go by. And the deeper we sink, so the harder we find it to escape, assuming indeed we even want to. Ideas which challenge our comfortable complacency are swiftly brushed aside, and before long a self-perpetuating cycle is established. Yet just occasionally something happens which throws everything, including our understanding of God, into the melting-pot. So it was for the prophet Ezekiel, faced suddenly with the painful prospect of exile into Babylon. Separated from his homeland, and with Jerusalem and the temple all too clearly heading for destruction, here was a crisis not just for him personally but for all his fellow-citizens taken into exile with him. How could God allow it happen? And how could faith make any sense of catastrophes such as these? The experience was deeply disturbing, but the divine encounter which resulted from it was to change Ezekiel's life for ever. God, he realised, was far greater than he had ever dared imagine; more wonderful than the mind can begin to fathom!

Reading – Ezekiel 1:1, 4-5a, 13, 15, 16b, 22, 26, 28

In the thirtieth year, in the fourth month, on the fifth day of the month, as I was among the exiles by the river Chebar, the heavens were opened, and I saw visions of God.

As I looked, a stormy wind came out of the north: a great cloud with brightness around it and fire flashing forth continually, and in the middle of the fire something like gleaming amber. In the middle of it was something like four living creatures. . . . In the middle of the living creatures there was something that looked like burning coals of fire, like torches moving to and fro among the living creatures; the fire was bright, and lightning issued from the fire.

As I looked at the living creatures, I saw a wheel on the earth beside the living creatures, one for each of the four of them . . . their construction being something like a wheel within a wheel.

Over the heads of the living creatures there was something like a dome, shining like crystal, spread out above their heads. . . . And above the dome over their heads there was something like a throne, in appearance like sapphire; and seated above the likeness of a throne was something that seemed like a human form.

Like the bow in a cloud on a rainy day, such was the appearance of
the splendour all around. This was the appearance of the likeness of
the glory of the Lord.

When I saw it, I fell on my face, and I heard the voice of someone
speaking.

Meditation

I thought I was an expert;
    that I, more than any, had glimpsed the wonder of God –
    his majesty,
    his power,
    his splendour.
I was a priest, you see,
    the temple my second home,
    and I'd worshipped there,
    sacrificed there,
    year after year,
    for as long as I could remember.
Surely I, of all people, should have understood his greatness?
Yet that day, by the river Chebar, I realised otherwise.
It was the last thing I expected,
    and the last place I'd have expected it;
    not Jerusalem,
    not even Judah,
    but a strange and distant country,
    land of foreign idols –
    Babylon!
Could God meet us there –
    his hand, his love, extend that far?
It seemed impossible,
    a vain and foolish dream,
    and I'd given it up long ago,
    dismissing it as so much fantasy.
He was holy, righteous,
    and we were steeped in sin,
    having wantonly and wilfully flouted his purpose;
    how then could he ever draw near,
    even had he wished to?
But suddenly, out of the blue, as I stood gazing homewards,
    I saw this vision,
    awesome,
    mysterious,
    God enthroned in glory,

sovereign over all.
I can't quite describe it,
    not as I want to,
    for there are no words sufficient,
    no pictures able to capture the wonder of that moment.
But there were tongues of fire and flashes of lightning,
    peals of thunder, rushing of wind,
    wheels within wheels, and wings touching wings,
    a rainbow of colour, whirlwind of sound.
And above it all, on a living chariot,
    moving now this way, now that,
    mighty, glorious, omnipotent,
    the Lord of hosts, ruler of heaven and earth,
    hidden in splendour.
It was staggering,
    incredible,
    and I fell down in homage,
    tears of joy filling my eyes;
    for he was *here*, seeking us out,
    as much God *here* in Babylon as anywhere else!
He had come to redeem us,
    to lead us home,
    no empire able to withstand his power,
    no people able to thwart his will.
Though *we* had failed him time and again,
    weak and foolish in so much,
    still he would not fail *us*.
I thought I was an expert,
    one who knew everything about God there was to know,
    but I'll never think that again, not for a moment,
    for I caught a glimpse of his greatness,
    just the merest glimmer, nothing more;
    and I'm still struggling to take even that in –
    that fleeting revelation –
    let alone to grasp the whole!

To ponder

- God moves in a mysterious way. *(William Cowper)*
- The nature of God is a circle of which the centre is everywhere and the circumference is nowhere. *(Attributed to Empedocles)*
- God is above all.
- Nor God alone in the still calm we find, he mounts the storm, and walks upon the wind. *(Alexander Pope)*

To discuss

- Christians today are sometimes accused of over-familiarity with God. Is this a danger? Have we lost our sense of awe and reverence and, if so, do we need to recover it?
- The idea of God as a bearded old man in the sky has long been laid to rest, but how do you picture God? Do you have the same sense of wonder which characterises the vision of Ezekiel?
- Ezekiel experienced his vision of God not in the temple of Jerusalem but far away from his homeland by the river Chebar in Babylon? Have there been times and places when you have been surprised by an unexpected sense of God's presence?

To consider further

Read Romans 11:33-36 and Colossians 1:11-20. Do we still catch our breath in wonder at the greatness of God revealed in Christ? Have we caught a glimpse of his glory, or brought the divine down to our own limited horizons?

Prayer

Gracious God,
    you are above all, beneath all,
    beyond all, within all.
You are God of past, present and future,
    of space and time, heaven and earth,
    all people, all creatures, all creation.
Forgive us that we lose sight of those awesome realities,
    settling instead for a fragmented picture of who you are
    shaped by our own narrow horizons,
    our flawed and limited understanding.
Save us from comfortable discipleship,
    from a faith which insulates us from your challenge
    rather than exposes us to your call.
Stir our imaginations,
    and help us to open our lives a little more each day
    to your great glory
    which is constantly waiting to surprise us.
In the name of Christ we pray.
Amen.

13 The last laugh

Obadiah

There's no getting away from it: within the Old Testament there's a strand of prophecy which is positively vindictive. We can do our best to sanitise their message by putting on it the best possible spiritual gloss, but the fact remains that we are dealing here with raw human emotion. It may not be pretty, but it is real and, above all, it is human. Perhaps that's why prophets like Obadiah make us feel uncomfortable; they hit a bit too close to home, reminding us of aspects of our own characters which we prefer to forget. Yet it is this very humanness which for me is one of the great strengths of the Old Testament, for it reminds us that God is able to speak through us despite our numerous flaws. So it is that Obadiah on the one hand displays a petty, if understandable, thirst for vengeance as he gleefully looks forward to the anticipated destruction of Edom; but on the other proclaims the enduring message of God's judgement on all those who fall victim to a misplaced sense of their own importance. It is worth pausing to reflect on both the man and the message, for there is probably a bit of Obadiah and Edom in each of us.

Reading – Obadiah 1-4, 12, 15b

The vision of Obadiah.
Thus says the Lord God concerning Edom:
We have heard a report from the Lord,
and a messenger has been sent among the nations:
'Rise up! Let us rise against it for battle!'
I will surely make you least among the nations;
you shall be utterly despised.
Your proud heart has deceived you,
you that live in the clefts of the rock,
whose dwelling is in the heights.
You say in your heart,
'Who will bring me down to the ground?'
Though you soar aloft like the eagle,
though your nest is set among the stars,
from there I will bring you down, says the Lord.
You should not have gloated over your brother

on the day of his misfortune;
you should not have rejoiced over the people of Judah
on the day of their ruin;
you should not have boasted on the day of distress.
As you have done, it shall be done to you;
your deeds shall return on your own head.

Meditation

Am I meant to feel sorry for them?
You think I should, don't you?
But I don't,
    and I won't –
    not even the merest hint of pity.
They've got it coming to them, that's how I see it,
    high time someone clipped their wings,
    for they've lorded it over their neighbours for too long,
    sneering at their misfortune,
    gloating over their downfall,
    gathering like vultures to pick greedily over the bones.
We know, for we've been there,
    suffering their looting and pillage for ourselves,
    violated in our hour of need.
Well, now it's their turn,
    and in my book they deserve whatever they get,
    no fate too harsh for them.
Yes, I know that seems hard,
    and there'll be plenty to condemn me for it, no doubt.
Show a bit of compassion, that's what they'll tell me;
    try seeing things from their point of view,
    forgive and forget.
Yet it's not that simple,
    for these people simply won't learn.
Day after day, year after year,
    they've rubbed our noses in the dust,
    sneering at our misfortune,
    and, to be frank, we've had our fill,
    fed up to the back teeth with their constant crowing.
So now that they're the ones facing humiliation,
    can you honestly blame us for feeling a touch smug?
They've been happy to dish it out;
    now the joke's on them,

and we can scarcely stop ourselves laughing.
Yes, we should know better, I don't dispute it,
  but remember this:
  it wasn't us who set them up for a fall;
  it was them –
  their own pride,
  their own greed,
  their own stupidity –
  so when the moment comes and they're brought low,
  don't be surprised when no one comes running to help them,
  least of all us –
  they've only themselves to blame.

To ponder

- Pride goes before, and shame follows after.
- Pride increases our enemies, but puts our friends to flight.
- Revenge is sweet.
- Revenge is a dish that can be eaten cold.
- Do as you would be done by.
- He that mischief hatches, mischief catches.

To discuss

- Are there times when we have wanted revenge? What were they? How did we cope with our feelings? Did we take vengeance or find a better way of dealing with the situation?
- It's natural sometimes to feel pleased when someone gets their come-uppance, but is it right? Is it asking too much to say we shouldn't have such feelings?
- Are we guilty sometimes of having an inflated opinion of ourselves, or of building ourselves up at the expense of others?

To consider further

Compare the teaching of Romans 12:14-21 with the message of Obadiah. What differences, and what parallels, do we see between the two?

Prayer

Gracious God,
> you tell us that as we forgive
> so we shall be forgiven,
> and the thought of that is frightening,
> for we find forgiving others so very difficult.

When we are hurt, insulted, let down,
> our natural inclination is to want revenge,
> and we allow that thirst to fester within us
> until it grows out of all proportion
> to the wrong we have suffered.

Teach us to leave vengeance to you,
> knowing that in your own time justice will be done.

Save us from that sense of bitterness within
> which finally will destroy *us* more than anyone.

Amen.

14 The God beyond us _____

Isaiah

There are few passages of Scripture which mean more to me than Isaiah 55:6-11. Why? Because these verses speak to the many and varied situations we find ourselves in as few others can, reminding us of the sheer 'otherness' of God, yet at the same time of his incredible grace. When life is hard to understand, when faith seems to fly in the face of reason, here is a reminder that behind the riddle of our fleeting existence lies a deeper purpose making sense of it all. When life is good, brimming over with promise, here is a testimony to the God who is able to bless us in ways untold and unimagined. When we're troubled by feelings of guilt and failure, convinced that no one in their right mind can possibly have time for us, we find here the assurance that he is always ready to forgive and forget, his grace defying human logic. So I could go on. These are verses which call us to a humble acknowledgement of our flawed knowledge of God, yet which speak simultaneously of the wonderful adventure of faith to which all are called; an adventure which this side of eternity can never end.

Reading – Isaiah 55:6-11

Seek the Lord while he may be found,
call upon him while he is near;
let the wicked forsake their way,
and the unrighteous their thoughts;
let them return to the Lord, that he may have mercy on them,
and to our God, for he will abundantly pardon.
For my thoughts are not your thoughts,
nor are your ways my ways, says the Lord.
For as the heavens are higher than the earth,
so are my ways higher than your ways
and my thoughts than your thoughts.
For as the rain and the snow come down from heaven,
and do not return there until they have fed and watered the earth,
making it bring forth and sprout,
giving seed to the sower and bread to the eater,
so shall my word be that goes out from my mouth;

it shall not return to me empty,
but it shall accomplish that which I purpose,
and succeed in the thing for which I sent it.

Meditation

I thought I knew him better than most,
    that over the years I'd come to understand him
    as few have even begun to.
And I suppose I had – to a point –
    for I'd glimpsed the wonder of his presence,
    I'd heard the sound of his voice,
    and, by his grace, I'd declared his purpose
    and made known his love:
    good news for all the world.
Impressed?
You shouldn't be –
    for it was nothing,
    just the merest glimmer of light,
    a tiny window on to an indescribable world of mystery.
Oh it was special, don't get me wrong,
    every moment of my ministry a privilege
    which I shall always treasure,
    shaping *my* life and that of countless others.
I spoke of love, and my heart thrilled within me,
    leaping like a deer sensing streams of life-giving water.
I spoke of forgiveness,
    a fresh start,
    new beginnings for us all,
    and my spirit sang for joy,
    dancing in exultation.
I spoke of light shining in the darkness,
    reaching out into the gloom,
    reviving, renewing, restoring,
    and my mouth gave praise to God,
    a song on my lips and his word on my tongue.
Yes, it was magical, no question,
    enough to set my soul on fire and my heart ablaze,
    yet it was a fraction of the whole,
    a speck of flotsam in the vast and unfathomable ocean
    that is God.

Whatever I'd glimpsed, far more lay hidden;
   whatever I'd grasped, far more had yet to be revealed,
   whatever I thought I'd understood,
   there was more always out of reach,
   too awesome even to contemplate,
   for we were different,
   he before all and over all, sovereign over space and time,
   and me? –
   a fleeting breath,
   a passing shadow,
   like the flower of the field, here today and gone tomorrow.
I thought I knew him, better than any,
   and to be fair, I did,
   my knowledge of him growing each day –
   new insights,
   new discoveries,
   new wonders beyond imagining,
   but I recognise now that, however far I've come,
   there's further still to go,
   more yet to learn –
   for all my travelling, the journey's only just begun!

To ponder

- Only a fool tries to get the heavens into his head; the wise man is quite content to get his head into the heavens. *(G. K. Chesterton, adapted)*
- Whereof one cannot speak, thereof one must be silent. *(Wittgenstein)*
- It is better to understand a little than to misunderstand a lot.
- The wise seek wisdom, a fool has found it.

To discuss

- Do we act sometimes as though God's ways and thoughts are like ours? How might we do this?
- Do we still see faith as a journey of discovery? How can we prevent ourselves from getting stuck in a rut?
- What are the dangers, for the Church and individual Christians, of losing sight of the otherness of God?

To consider further

Read John 1:1-18. In what way does the revelation of God in Christ affect our interpretation of Isaiah's words?

Prayer

Sovereign God,
    all too often we have lost sight of your greatness,
    settling instead for a picture of you we feel comfortable with.
We have frustrated your will
    through the smallness of our vision.
We have missed opportunities to serve you
    through the narrowness of our horizons.
We have denied ourselves your mercy
    through the confines we place upon your grace.
Time and again we have presumed
    that your ways are *our* ways
    and your thoughts *our* thoughts,
    forgetting that you are beyond words
    or human understanding.
Forgive us,
    and teach us never to underestimate
    the awesomeness of your being
    or the extent of your love.
Amen.

15 First things first _____

Haggai

We live today, so we are told, in an age of rampant materialism; an era in which everyone is always grasping after the newest gadget, the latest fashion, the most up-to-date model. It is difficult to argue with such an assessment of modern society, but is the phenomenon as new as we sometimes tend to make out? The book of Haggai suggests not. As we read through its pages, we could well be reading a socio-economic analysis of Britain today, such are the similarities in tone. The technology and resources at our disposal may be far greater than those in Haggai's time, but the underlying cravings are no different. Greed, materialism, call it what you will, is an age-old, and probably universal, characteristic, yet the irony is that it rarely seems to bring happiness, all too often indeed the reverse. Creature comforts have their place, as Haggai would, I'm sure, have been the first to accept, but if we put these before our spiritual needs, the result is a never-ending striving for an inner fulfilment which will for ever remain tantalisingly out of reach.

Reading – Haggai 1:1-9

In the second year of King Darius, in the sixth month, on the first day of the month, the word of the Lord came by the prophet Haggai to Zerubbabel son of Shealtiel, governor of Judah, and to Joshua son of Jehozadak, the high priest. Thus says the Lord of hosts: These people say the time has not yet come to rebuild the Lord's house. Then the word of the Lord came by the prophet Haggai, saying: Is it a time for you yourselves to live in panelled houses, while this house lies in ruins? Now therefore thus says the Lord of hosts: Consider how you have fared. You have sown much, and harvested little; you eat, but you never have enough; you drink, but you never have your fill; you clothe yourselves, but no one is warm; and you that earn wages earn wages to put them into a bag with holes.

Thus says the Lord of hosts: Consider how you have fared. Go up to the hills and bring wood and build the house, so that I may take pleasure in it and be honoured, says the Lord. You have looked for much, and, lo, it came to little; and when you brought it home, I blew it away. Why? says the Lord of hosts. Because my house lies in ruins, while all of you hurry off to your own houses.

Meditation

I could hardly believe what I was seeing;
    quite honestly, it left me speechless!
After all we'd been through,
    everything God had done for us,
    to ignore him so brazenly –
    it was beyond belief.
Yet there they were,
    building bigger and better homes for themselves each day,
    and not a thought for the house of God
    lying in ruins just a few yards from their door.
You'd have thought they'd have learned their lesson, wouldn't you? –
    those interminable years in Babylon
    enough to bring anyone to their senses –
    but not them, I'm afraid;
    it was just like it had always been,
    self first
    God second.
Only they didn't seem to realise it, that's the strange thing;
    they honestly felt hard done by,
    cheated, somehow, as their dreams turned to ashes,
    and their hopes lay trodden in the dust.
'What's happened?' they asked me.
'Why has God brought us back, only to withhold his blessing?'
Incredible, I know, yet true!
Couldn't they see it was their own fault,
    the result of their own folly?
Apparently not.
Yet it should have been clear to anyone
    that a society based on greed –
    on looking after number one and never mind the rest –
    could only end one way,
    in utter rack and ruin.
It grieved me to see it,
    but it grieved God far more,
    for once again he saw his people frittering away
    the riches he'd given,
    squandering his precious gift of life.
Would it all end in tears, once more?
It nearly did,
    but, thankfully, this time when he spoke,
    they were ready to listen,
    ready to learn,

and ready to change.
If only you could see us now,
    what a difference it's made!
We're not just a country again,
    a group of exiles restored to our homeland –
    we're a community,
    a nation,
    a people united in faith.
I'm not saying everything's perfect, our troubles over,
    for I've no doubt there will be more mistakes
    and more trials to face,
    but we realise now that there's more to life
    than our own interests,
    more to this world than self;
    and the irony is, in giving God his rightful place,
    we've discovered our own worth too,
    and the worth of everyone, and everything, around us.

To ponder

- He is a slave of the greatest slave, who serves nothing but himself.
- We are not born for ourselves.
- Grasp all, lose all.
- The more you get, the more you want.
- Covetousness brings nothing home.

To discuss

- What gadget or 'mod con' have you bought recently? Why did you buy it? Has it brought the benefits/pleasures you expected?
- How important are possessions to you? Which do you regard as essential? Which could you happily do without?
- Do you think giving to God should be an integral part of your weekly budget? What are your views on the principle of tithing?
- Have we ever found that material possessions leave us feeling poorer, and the loss of them richer? If so, in what way?

To consider further

Read Matthew 6:19-34. The words sound wonderful, but in what ways, if at all, do we apply them to our lives? Is it time you reassessed your priorities in living and giving?

Prayer

Lord,
  you have given to us without counting the cost.
Forgive us that we find it so hard to give back to you.
We intend to respond,
  but we are enslaved to self,
    our own interests constantly thrusting themselves forward
    until they blot out all else.
Teach us to recognise the road to true fulfilment,
  to understand that unless we are willing
  to lose everything we have,
  we will never finally find anything worth having.
Teach us to let go of self
  and, in serving you and others,
  to discover the life you freely offer us,
  brimming over beyond measure.
Amen.

16 Daring to hope

Zechariah

To have our hopes raised only to see them dashed again is a cruel experience. The result can be to plunge us into a deeper sense of despair than anything we faced previously. So it was for the people of Israel after they returned to Judah following their time of exile in Babylon. An initial mood of jubilation soon gave way to an over-whelming feeling of anticlimax, as the Utopia which people had expected failed to materialise. It wasn't just hope which took a battering in consequence; for many it was their faith. Where was the glorious new kingdom God had promised his people? Today the kingdom we expect may be different, but the question can seem equally valid. We look forward to the day when God's purpose will be fulfilled, when his will shall be done and his kingdom come on earth. But when will that be? Do we have the courage to keep on hoping, even when everything around us seems to undermine belief?

Reading – Zechariah 14:1, 6-9

See, a day is coming for the Lord, when the plunder taken from you will be divided in your midst.

On that day there shall not be either cold or frost. And there shall be continuous day (it is known to the Lord), not day and not night, for at evening time there shall be light.

On that day living waters shall flow out from Jerusalem, half of them to the eastern sea and half of them to the western sea; it shall continue in summer as in winter.

And the Lord will become king over all the earth; on that day the Lord will be one and his name one.

Meditation

Was it worth continuing?
Could we go on any longer closing our eyes to the truth?
It was hard not to ask that,
    as, once more, our hopes came to nothing.

We thought we'd turned the corner
    after the traumas and turmoil of exile –
    a new beginning to blot away the memory
    of those interminable years,
    so hard to bear, so bitter to remember.
Not that we were treated badly there, we could never say that,
    but there was always a sense of emptiness,
    the knowledge that we were far from home;
    far from the land of our fathers and the city of God.
We could never forget that, try though we might,
    so when the chance came to return,
    you can imagine, we grasped it,
    beside ourselves with joy,
    looking forward with eager expectation
    to a bright new era,
    God's kingdom, here on earth.
Only it didn't happen that way.
After the initial euphoria came the harsh reality –
    the magnitude of the challenge before us,
    and the feebleness of our resources to meet it.
We did our best, of course –
    little by little restoring the temple –
    but it soon became clear to everyone,
    even the most optimistic,
    that we could never regain past glories,
    let alone surpass them.
It was a question of making do,
    getting by as best we could –
    the sooner we reconciled ourselves to second best,
    the better for everyone.
I thought the same until today, I have to admit it,
    my despair and disillusionment as keen as anyone's.
But not any more,
    for God granted me last night an astonishing vision,
    a picture of a glorious new kingdom
    unlike any I've seen before.
I saw a new dawn, bathing the world in light,
    the sun rising ever higher, warm upon my face,
    shimmering across streams of living water,
    sparkling upon fields wet with dew.
I saw a new creation at one with itself,
    a land reflecting God's love and mercy,
    with him there at the centre,

ruling in splendour,
   all in all.
I saw a kingdom of justice and truth,
   sorrow a thing of the past,
   despair consigned to history,
   our cup running over with good things.
And my spirit leapt,
   dancing in joyful celebration!
We're not there yet, not by a long way,
   but God has given us a glimpse of things to come,
   a taste of paradise;
   and we're resolved now to keep going,
   however long it may take us,
   whatever the setbacks,
   until the day we enter that kingdom,
   and see his glory,
   more wonderful than we can ever imagine!

To ponder

- A good hope is better than a bad possession.
- In the land of hope there is never any winter.
- Bear with evil and expect good.
- The darkest hour is that before dawn.

To discuss

- Should we pin all our hopes on some future kingdom, or does faith give grounds for hope in this life too?
- Is there any difference between optimism, hope and wishful thinking? If so, what is it?
- In what ways does the Christian faith bring hope?

To consider further

Read Revelation 21:1-6. Take heart from God's promise that his kingdom will come.

Prayer

Sovereign God,
>   you have promised that the time will come
>   when your kingdom will be established,
>   your people rejoice in the wonder of your love
>   and all creation celebrate your goodness.

It is this prospect
>   which inspires us to new endeavours of faith
>   and which gives us strength in times of adversity,
>   yet there are times, if we are honest,
>   when the vision starts to fade.

Confronted by the harsh realities of life,
>   we wonder sometimes if it makes sense
>   to keep on believing.

Assure us in such moments that, despite appearances,
>   you are there
>   and that, in the fullness of time,
>   your will shall triumph and our hope be vindicated.

Amen.

17 Studying the word _____

_____ *Ezra*

Few people if asked to list their top ten characters of the Old Testament would include Ezra in their choice. Despite having a book named after him, he fails to capture the imagination in the way that characters like Moses, Samson, David or Isaiah do. Some have called him dull; others have gone even further and accused him of being largely responsible for the narrow legalism which came to typify Judaism at the time of Jesus. Yet this is to overlook the very real contribution Ezra made to his nation at a formative time in its history, and to undervalue the motivation which lay behind it. As a scribe and priest his overriding concern was to nurture the faith of his people, and he did this in the way he knew best. There is much we could learn today from his example of single-minded devotion to the study of God's word.

Reading – Ezra 7:6-10

Ezra went up from Babylonia. He was a scribe skilled in the law of Moses that the Lord the God of Israel had given; and the king granted him all that he asked, for the hand of the Lord his God was upon him.

Some of the people of Israel, and some of the priests and Levites, the singers and gatekeepers, and the temple servants also went up to Jerusalem, in the seventh year of King Artaxerxes. They came to Jerusalem in the fifth month, which was in the seventh year of the king. On the first day of the first month the journey up from Babylon was begun, and on the first day of the fifth month he came to Jerusalem, for the gracious hand of his God was upon him. For Ezra had set his heart to study the law of the Lord, and to do it, and to teach the statutes and ordinances in Israel.

Meditation

I didn't have much to offer, I knew that –
    no extravagant gifts,
    no stunning insights –
    just a love of God
    and a desire to serve him as best I could.
So I made it my goal to study his word,
    to read sentence by sentence the book of the law.
    so that I might know his will
    and help rebuild our nation.
Nothing dramatic, true – still less glamorous –
    but it was something I could do,
    and a job that needed doing.
Why?
Because I'd seen for myself
    what forgetting God could lead to,
    the tragic results of flouting his will
    and ignoring his commandments.
I'd been there in Babylon, remember,
    sharing my people's exile,
    enduring the frustration and heartache
    of being far from the land of our fathers,
    cut off from the city of God;
    and if there was one thing I'd resolved during that time,
    it was this:
    never, never again!
So I read, and kept on reading,
    hour after hour,
    day after day,
    until my head throbbed and my eyes ached,
    no detail too small,
    no point too trivial,
    everything noted and stored carefully away.
It was an obsession, I admit it,
    but, you see, this was to be a fresh start for our people,
    a bright new chapter in our history,
    and I was determined we shouldn't waste it.
We'd paid the price for past mistakes,
    but had we learned our lesson?
There was only one way to be sure.
Did I take it too far?
Some would say so,
    and, yes, they're probably right,

for anything can be abused, even God's word,
and through my emphasis on the fine print
I fear I may have obscured the whole picture.
It's not the words that matter but the message,
the spirit rather than letter of the law,
and if you get that wrong, then better not to read at all.
But that's finally down to you, not me.
I've given the tools, as best I can;
it's up to you to use them.

To ponder

- Thinking is the essence of wisdom. *(Persian proverb)*
- The devil can cite Scripture for his purpose. *(William Shakespeare)*
- Study without reflection is a waste of time; reflection without study is dangerous. *(Confucius)*

To discuss

- Which passages of the Bible do you like to read most and which least? Why?
- What sort of things prevent us from making time for regular Bible study? When we do find time, what do we find hardest about understanding the words we're reading?
- If it's true that 'the devil can cite Scripture for his purpose', is it possible that we can unintentionally misuse the Bible? In what ways? Are we sometimes more interested in the letter than the spirit, or do we go too far the other way?
- What are the dangers of reading and quoting passages of Scripture out of context? How important is it to understand the situations in which different books of the Bible were written? Do we make time to learn about these?

To consider further

Read 2 Timothy 3:10-17. Make time to grapple with *all* Scripture rather than just selected bits of it. Don't settle for a faith which says more about *you* than *God*.

Prayer

Living God,
    you have given us your word in the Scriptures,
    but all too often we fail to read them.
We dip in casually as the mood takes us,
    selecting those bits which suit us best
    and ignoring the passages
    which might prove difficult or demanding.
Even the little we read is rarely applied to our lives
    in a way that really touches them.
Despite the claims we make for it,
    the reality is that much of the Bible is a closed book to us.
Forgive us,
    and help us make time and space in our lives
    to study your word,
    to hear you speaking,
    and to respond in faith.
Amen.

18 Out of sight, out of mind?

Nehemiah

The book of Nehemiah is not an easy book to read. It displays an antipathy towards so-called 'foreigners' which borders on the xeno-phobic, coupled with a chilling level of religious intolerance. Yet when we recall the persecution the Jews had already suffered countless times in their history up to this point, we can begin to understand the reasoning behind Nehemiah's apparent paranoia. Not only this, but exposure to outside influences had led in the past to a steady dilution of his people's faith; a slow but inexorable compromise of principles and convictions. In our modern-day cosmopolitan and multi-faith society, we can well understand such tensions. But if these were a problem for Nehemiah, there was something which troubled him more; namely a crushing sense of guilt as the sufferings of his distant kinfolk back in Israel became known to him. His swift response to their plight provides a powerful challenge to us, not just with respect to the needs of our fellow-citizens, which all too often may be pushed conveniently to the back of our minds, but also to the sufferings of the wider world, which today cannot be ignored, however much we try to escape them.

Reading – Nehemiah 1:1-7

The words of Nehemiah son of Hacaliah. In the month of Chislev, in the twentieth year, while I was in Susa the capital, one of my brothers, Hanani, came with certain men from Judah; and I asked them about the Jews that survived, those who had escaped the captivity, and about Jerusalem. They replied, 'The survivors there in the province who escaped captivity are in great trouble and shame; the wall of Jerusalem is broken down, and its gates have been destroyed by fire.'

When I heard these words I sat down and wept, and mourned for days, fasting and praying before the God of heaven. I said, 'O Lord God of heaven, the great and awesome God who keeps covenant and steadfast love with those who love him and keep his commandments; let your ear be attentive and your eyes open to hear the prayer of your servant that I now pray before you day and night for your servants, the people of Israel, confessing the sins of the people of Israel, which we have sinned against you. Both I and my family have sinned. We have offended you deeply, failing to keep the commandments, the statutes, and the ordinances that you commanded your servant Moses.'

Meditation

I knew things had been bad back in Jerusalem,
 we all did, every man, woman and child.
Never mind that we'd never been there –
 we'd heard the stories too many times to be in any doubt:
 how the soldiers had marched in,
 demolishing the walls and torching the city,
 looting, raping and pillaging,
 before carrying off the cream of the nation into exile
 while the rest were left to fend for themselves.
Our hearts had bled for them at first,
 the dreadful images those stories conjured up
 haunting us day and night,
 and we were resolved never to forget
 nor forgive those dreadful deeds.
But it was long ago now,
 and as the dust had settled, so we had settled with it,
 the strange land of Babylon not so dreadful after all,
 offering to those with the wit to take them, rich rewards
 and swift advancement;
 good homes,
 good jobs,
 good prospects.
We still *believed* we cared,
 still even called Jerusalem 'home'
 in a romantic sort of way,
 but for most of us it had become just a name,
 promising much,
 signifying little.
I was as guilty as any, I'm afraid,
 for life had worked out well for me –
 a trusted position at court,
 the king's own cup-bearer –
 what reason was there to rock the boat?
Only, then, my brother turned up, fresh from Jerusalem,
 and suddenly the whole sorry picture was laid bare before me –
 the squalor,
 the suffering,
 the misery of a once-proud people in a once-proud city
 brought to abject ruin,
 an object of ridicule to all around them.
How did I feel?
I was overcome – there's no other word for it –

not just with sorrow, but shame,
    for in my own way I was as responsible as any,
    their hopelessness, at least in part, down to me.
Ostensibly a victim, I had become one of the victors,
    ensconced in my comfortable home,
    secure and respected,
    the needs of those outside, even my own people,
    quietly swept under the carpet.
It hadn't been done consciously,
    still less planned,
    but it had happened nonetheless,
    and the truth hurt, more than I can tell.
What did I do?
I went back, of course,
    using my influence, as God surely intended I should,
    to secure safe passage home,
    and the resources needed to help them start afresh.
You should see it now,
    it's a different place –
    the walls rebuilt,
    the city restored,
    the future beckoning;
    but I'm haunted once again,
    unable to forget that dreadful moment
    when our failure was exposed –
    a moment which taught me that it's one thing to think you care;
    to believe someone, somewhere, matters;
    quite another when it comes to proving it.

To ponder

- God himself is the help of the helpless. *(Indian proverb)*
- Slow help is no help.
- When need is highest, help is nighest.
- Example is better than precept.
- There is a sin of omission as well as commission.

To discuss

- The local church is often described as a family of Christians. How realistic is this description? In what sense should we be a family, and how far do we live up to that?
- Is there a danger sometimes of being so wrapped up in church activities that we overlook the needs of the wider fellowship?
- How ready are we to offer concrete help to others, rather than simply words? Is there a danger of so spiritualising the Gospel that it becomes all talk rather than action?

To consider further

Read Romans 15:25-29, 2 Corinthians 9:1-15 and Galatians 6:7-10. Resolve to put your faith into practice this week by offering some practical help to family and friends. Don't just think about it; do it!

Prayer

Living God,
    we talk of being a light to the nations,
    of reaching out with your love to the ends of the earth,
    but sometimes we do not even get
    as far as those on our own doorstep.
For all our high ideals,
    we fail to recognise the great family to which we belong,
    our concern more for ourselves or our own immediate circle
    than the wider world.
Forgive us for the many times we have failed you
    through the narrowness of our vision,
    and give us sensitivity
    to the needs of our brothers and sisters in Christ,
    and a willingness to respond to people everywhere.
In his name we pray.
Amen.

19 Food for our souls _____

_____ *Joel*

The words of Joel 2:26-32 must be some of the most often quoted in the whole of Scripture. Yet how many of us have ever actually read for ourselves this little book tucked away towards the end of the Old Testament? Probably very few, and that's a pity, for the context in which these verses are set makes both the promise within them, and its ultimate fulfilment, all the more wonderful. Joel spoke to a nation which was both physically and spiritually emaciated. A plague of locusts had brought widespread devastation and consequent famine, yet for the prophet this was just a symbol of a much deeper emptiness – a barrenness of soul. The people of Judah had turned their backs on God, no longer believing he had any relevance to their daily lives, no longer expecting him to speak or act in human history. Think again, says Joel. God is able to fill not only body but spirit, meeting our innermost needs and touching every part of our lives. For us today the fulfilment of those words is seen in the coming of the Holy Spirit at Pentecost, the gift of power from on high. That Spirit is at work in the lives of all, recognised or unrecognised. Are we ready to open our lives and let God shape us and fill us as he will?

Reading – Joel 2:12-14, 26-32

Even now, says the Lord,
return to me with all your heart,
with fasting, with weeping, and with mourning;
rend your hearts and not your clothing.
Return to the Lord, your God,
for he is gracious and merciful,
slow to anger, and abounding in steadfast love,
and relents from punishing.
Who knows whether he will turn and relent,
and leave a blessing behind him,
a grain offering and a drink offering
for the Lord, your God?
You shall eat in plenty and be satisfied,
and praise the name of the Lord your God,
who has dealt wondrously with you.
And my people shall never again be put to shame.
You shall know that I am in the midst of Israel,

and that I, the Lord, am your God and there is no other.
And my people shall never again be put to shame.
Then afterwards I will pour out my spirit on all flesh;
your sons and your daughters shall prophesy,
your old men shall dream dreams,
and your young men shall see visions.
Even on the male and female slaves,
in those days, I will pour out my spirit.
I will show portents in the heavens and on the earth,
blood and fire and columns of smoke.
The sun shall be turned to darkness,
and the moon to blood,
before the great and terrible day of the Lord comes.
Then everyone who calls on the name of the Lord
shall be saved;
for in Mount Zion and in Jerusalem
there shall be those who escape, as the Lord has said,
and among the survivors shall be those whom the Lord calls.

Meditation

It had been a hard time by anyone's standards –
    a famine like no other we'd known before,
    cruel,
    savage,
    merciless;
    sapping our strength,
    gnawing at our bellies –
    enough to test the faith of the most devoted.
We felt close to breaking, each one of us,
    such hunger hard to bear,
    yet strangely it was a different emptiness
    that should have concerned us –
    not the hollowness in our stomachs
    but a far greater void:
    the barrenness of our faith,
    the aridity of our lives,
    spirits emaciated by lack of sustenance.
Here was the true threat to our future.
We understood those pangs in our stomach,
    knew them for what they were,
    but that dull ache deep within,
    that remorseless craving;
    it left us tortured,

bewildered,
conscious of our need yet at a loss how to meet it.
If anything showed the measure of our fall, that was it;
for all the time God was there,
prompting,
pleading,
longing to fill our stricken souls;
only we would not or could not see it.
And that's how it might have ended were it not for his grace,
had he, in his mercy, not decreed otherwise.
But in love he kept on calling,
speaking his word,
offering his promise –
a new era,
a new kingdom which he would bring to pass.
Not just food and plenty, though that was gift enough,
but his spirit deep within!
And not just for some, the chosen few,
but all –
young and old,
man and woman,
slave and free,
rich and poor!
It was unheard of,
unthinkable,
a picture exceeding all our expectations –
surely too good to be true?
Yet that's what he told us,
the time coming when our sons and daughters will prophesy,
our old men dream dreams and the young see visions,
when all flesh will know the indwelling of his presence.
Can it be true?
I still wonder sometimes,
for can he really touch not just one life but so many,
transforming what *is* into what he would have it be?
It seems impossible,
only I've tasted his power for myself,
experienced the renewal his spirit brings,
and I know now that not only *can* it be –
it *has* to be –
for then, and only then, can we find the nourishment we need
and the fulfilment we crave –
food to feed our souls!

To ponder

- The wind blows where it chooses, and you hear the sound of it, but you do not know where it comes from or where it goes. So it is with everyone who is born of the spirit. *(John 3:8)*
- The awful shadow of some unseen Power floats though unseen among us. *(Percy Bysshe Shelley)*

To discuss

- Joel speaks of God pouring out his spirit on all flesh. Is our picture of the Spirit's movement too narrow sometimes, tied down to the way we expect God to work?
- 'Dreaming dreams and seeing visions.' What do you think Joel meant by this? Do we have a vision for the future, for our church and for the world? What is it?
- What do you believe are signs of the Holy Spirit's activity?

To consider further

Read Matthew 5:6 and Romans 12:3-8. Have we allowed the Holy Spirit freedom to work in our lives? Are we open to the Spirit's movement in the lives of those around us?

Prayer

Gracious God,
    we thank you that whoever we are,
    whatever our age, sex, colour or background,
    we can know you for ourselves
    through the living presence of your Holy Spirit.
We thank you that you meet our innermost needs,
    filling our empty souls to overflowing
    through that Spirit's power.
Come to us now,
    and help us to dream dreams and see visions.
Help us to catch a new sense of all you have done,
    all you are doing, and all you have yet to do.
In the name of Christ.
Amen.

20 The moment of truth

Malachi

Ask somebody to name the last book of the Old Testament and the chances are they may well come up with the book of Malachi. Ask them to tell you what the book is about, and you will almost certainly find a response less forthcoming. Like the other so-called 'minor prophets', we may recognise the name but the book remains firmly closed. Yet anyone who has ever listened to Handel's great choral masterpiece *Messiah* will have heard at least something of this prophet's words, for there we find set to music Malachi's chilling challenge concerning the Messiah's coming. The words make sobering reading, not least because those they were first addressed to were convinced they were more than ready for that moment, and assured of divine approval when it finally happened. From Malachi came the call to think again – to examine their consciences, assess their lifestyles, and ask themselves whether everything was quite as it should be. Many were in for a shock. The same can be true for us today if we allow ourselves to become complacent or stale in our faith. Malachi reminds us of the constant need to grapple honestly and openly with God, responding afresh each day to his challenge.

Reading – Malachi 2:17-3:3a, 5

You have wearied the Lord with your words. Yet you say, 'How have we wearied him?' By saying, 'All who do evil are good in the sight of the Lord, and he delights in them.' Or by asking, 'Where is the God of justice?'

See, I am sending my messenger to prepare the way before me, and the Lord whom you seek will suddenly come to his temple. The messenger of the covenant in whom you delight – indeed, he is coming, says the Lord of hosts. But who can endure the day of his coming, and who can stand when he appears?

For he is like a refiner's fire and like fullers' soap; he will sit as a refiner and purifier of silver, and he will purify the descendants of Levi. I will draw near to you for judgement; I will be swift to bear witness against the sorcerers, against the adulterers, against those who swear falsely, against those who oppress the hired workers in their wages, the widow and the orphan, against those who thrust aside the alien, and do not fear me, says the Lord of hosts.

Meditation

Not long now, they tell me –
    just a little longer and the day will come,
    the Messiah arrive –
    a new era,
    the dawn of a wonderful new age,
    God's kingdom here on earth,
    with us, his chosen people, right at the centre of it!
No more suffering,
    no more smarting under the yoke of occupation,
    but freedom,
    prosperity,
    blessings too many to number!
That's what they tell me, anyway –
    what they're all expecting.
If only they knew!
If only they could see themselves as they really are,
    perhaps then they'd change their tune.
For I tell you this, they've got it horribly wrong,
    each way off the mark and heading for a terrible let-down.
Oh he's coming all right, the Messiah, no doubt about that –
    maybe not in my lifetime,
    maybe not in theirs –
    but he's coming, just as they say.
Only it won't be the party some seem to imagine –
    not a bit of it.
Why?
Do you really have to ask?
Just look around at the mess we're in,
    the state of our society,
    the shallowness of our lifestyles.
Can you see the Messiah giving us a pat on the back
    when he sees it all?
I can't.
He'll be shocked, more likely,
    dismayed at the way we've failed so miserably
    to prepare for his coming,
    and I can't see him turning a blind eye,
    no matter who we are.
I wish I could say different.
Truly, I'd love to believe I'm mistaken,
    that we're ready and waiting for his coming.
But we're nowhere near it,

nowhere near it at all.
Let them look forward if they want to.
Let them pray for the day of the Lord.
I only hope, before he answers us,
    that God gives us time to take a long hard look at ourselves,
    get our house in order
    and ask just who it is we're expecting,
    for otherwise,
    when the day finally arrives,
    I have this grim foreboding
    that many crying out now to see him come,
    will end up doing all they can to see him gone.

To ponder

- Truth will out.
- Poison is poison though it comes in a golden cup.
- Vice is often clothed in virtue's habit.
- Straight trees have crooked roots.
- A holy habit cleanses not a foul soul.

To discuss

- There were many in Malachi's day who believed they were faithful yet found themselves condemned by the prophet's message. Religion had got in the way of faith. In what ways can the same thing happen today?
- Which are we best at: serving others or serving self? Is the faith we profess on Sunday evident in our lives during the rest of the week?

To consider further

Read Mark 13:26-37. What things in your life would you be most ashamed of if Jesus were to return today?

Prayer

Lord,
    you call us to test ourselves
    and ensure that we are still in the faith.
Help us to take that challenge seriously,
    for it is all too easy to imagine everything is well
    when in fact we've lost our way.
We may still follow you outwardly,
    but in our hearts be far from you,
    our love grown cold.
Save us, we pray,
    from the ever-present danger of complacency.
Draw us closer to you, day by day,
    so that our faith may always be as real and as fresh
    as the day we first believed.
Prepare us for your coming again in Christ,
    so that we may be ready to receive him
    and found faithful in his service.
In his name we pray.
Amen.

Final prayer

Living God,
 for all the times we have wrestled against you,
 flouting your will,
 ignoring your call,
 disobeying your commandments,
 resisting your guidance,
 forgive us.

In all the times we wrestle with you,
 striving to understand more,
 searching for meaning,
 grappling with our unbelief,
 begging for your help,
 hear us.

In all the times we wrestle in faith,
 seeking to do your will,
 working towards your kingdom,
 committing ourselves to your service,
 confronting evil and injustice in your name,
 bless us.

Teach us not to contend *against* you
 but to work *with* you,
 to grapple earnestly with the great mysteries of faith,
 and to give of ourselves freely in the cause of Christ.

Go with us we pray,
 and may your word live within us,
 a lamp for our path
 and a fire on our tongue,
 to the glory of your name.
Amen.

Index of Bible passages _____

(References are to meditation rather than page numbers)

Index of principal characters _____

Index of principal themes _____